IN THE TWILIGHT OF THE CHRISTIAN WEST

In the Twilight
of the Christian West

*A Theology of Mourning
and Resistance*

MAC LOFTIN

ORBIS BOOKS
Maryknoll, New York

Library of Congress Cataloging-in-Publication Data

Names: Loftin, Mac author
Title: In the twilight of the Christian West : a theology of mourning
   and resistance / Mac Loftin.
Description: Maryknoll, NY : Orbis Books, [2025] | Includes bibliographical
   references. | Summary: "Counters the Christian right's theology of power
   by recovering antifascist theological voices that embrace liberative
   mourning to forge resistance in troubling times"—Provided by publisher.
Identifiers: LCCN 2025019765 (print) | LCCN 2025019766 (ebook) |
   ISBN 9781626986329 trade paperback | ISBN 9798888660874 epub
Subjects: LCSH: Christianity and politics | Grief—Religious aspects |
   Fascism
Classification: LCC BR115.P7 L577 2025 (print) | LCC BR115.P7 (ebook) |
   DDC 261.7—dc23/eng/20250610
LC record available at https://lccn.loc.gov/2025019765
LC ebook record available at https://lccn.loc.gov/2025019766

To Cleo

ὡσεὶ κυβερνήτας σοφός, ὑμνοάνασσ᾽
εὔθυνε Κλειοῖ
νῦν φρένας ἁμετέρας,
εἰ δή ποτε καὶ πάρος

—BACCHYLIDES

*What can oppose the decline of the West
is not a resurrected culture but the utopia
that is silently contained in
the image of its decline.*

—THEODOR ADORNO

*And above all in Christendom,
the fewer the better!*

—SØREN KIERKEGAARD

Contents

Introduction

In May 1944, in a Wehrmacht barracks in the town of Velletri just outside Rome, a German soldier named Eberhard Bethge woke up to a stack of letters on his bunk. He thumbed through the pile until he found one, folded and stained but otherwise nondescript. Like the ones before, there was nothing suspicious about it, nothing that gave it away as having been smuggled out of a military prison. Bethge discreetly turned away from the other men as he pulled out a knife and opened the envelope. His friend Dietrich Bonhoeffer was always careful; Bethge knew the letter would say nothing of the plans in motion to assassinate the Führer, but still. Better to be safe. He slid the letter out and read slowly. Whether to savor it or avoid it he couldn't say. He had always enjoyed watching the mind of his friend, the brilliant theologian, at work. But lately that mind had turned strange. Bonhoeffer's letters had pushed to the edge of theological thinking and kept pushing. It was like the void of the prison cell was leaking into the letters. Bonhoeffer still wrote about God, but God in his letters had become weak, powerless, suffering, dead, gone.

Folded in the envelope was a sermon Bonhoeffer had agreed to write for Bethge's newborn son. Bethge had hoped the task would cheer Bonhoeffer up, would be a channel for the other mood that flowed just as often from his letters, the lust for life and experience that the prison guards and air raids had not yet been able to destroy. Bethge smiled at the dedication: "Thoughts on the Day of Baptism of Dietrich Wilhelm Rüdiger Bethge." But as he read his smile faded and his brow knit together. This was more than a baptism sermon for his son. It was a funeral sermon for Christianity itself.

Bonhoeffer had been asked to welcome little Dietrich Bethge into the Christian faith, but, as the sermon made clear, in his eyes Christianity in the West had been so bankrupted by its complicity with fascism—the doglike obedience in Germany, the studied silence everywhere else—that nothing remained of it but ruins. The water poured on the child's head would also be dirt thrown on the grave of Christendom.

What led the Christian West down the path of cowardly silence if not enthusiastic participation, Bonhoeffer wrote in the sermon, was the fear that a familiar form of Christian life was on the brink of disappearing. "Our church has been fighting during these years only for its self-preservation," he lamented.[1] Christians in Germany, fearing the end of Christian faith at the hands of either secular liberals or godless communists, had embraced the Nazis as their last, best hope for survival. In Bonhoeffer's eyes, this attempt to preserve Christianity at all costs had itself snuffed out the possibility of genuine faith. Nazism, Bonhoeffer wrote shortly after Hitler took power and the churches folded to his will, "brought an end to the church in Germany."[2] The rest of Christianity in the West, so silent in the face of the Shoah, fared no better. Bonhoeffer's sermon declared the church "has become incapable of bringing the Word of reconciliation and redemption to humankind and the world." The church's task was now to silence itself: "The words we used before must fall silent and become powerless." Silent and powerless, Christian communities could no longer pretend to bring a saving word to the non-Western, non-Christian world. Instead they must listen for that word to be spoken to them by that world. The Word will speak again, but "in a new language, perhaps quite nonreligious language."[3] Bonhoeffer

1. Dietrich Bonhoeffer, *Letters and Papers from Prison*, ed. John W. De Gruchy; trans. Isabel Best et al.; Dietrich Bonhoeffer Works 8 (Minneapolis: Fortress Press, 2010), 389.

2. Dietrich Bonhoeffer, *Gesammelte Schriften* (Munich: Christian Kaiser Verlag, 1958), 1:39–40.

3. Bonhoeffer, *Letters and Papers from Prison*, 389–90.

argued that if there was any hope for Christianity after its complicity with fascism, it could paradoxically only be found by Christianity letting go of itself. Christians, he insisted, must refuse the temptation to cling to the familiar at all costs, and instead open ourselves to being transformed by those different from us, listening in attentive silence to the strange and unfamiliar words of strange and unfamiliar peoples as perhaps the Word we seek. Christians must learn to mourn the inevitable loss of our beloved and familiar way of life. Only by doing so might we discover what that life was about all along. What is needed, Bonhoeffer wrote in words he would never say over a child he would never baptize, is a Christianity capable of mourning its own death.

※

Elsewhere in his letters to Bethge, Bonhoeffer railed against psychoanalysis. Charlatans like Freud, he complained, convince healthy people they're sick only to turn around and sell analysis as the cure. In these letters Bonhoeffer sounded just like his father, Karl Bonhoeffer, the former head of the psychiatry department at Friedrich Wilhelm University, who tried to exorcize Freud like a ghost from the department. But as any analyst could have predicted, Dietrich's reaction against psychoanalysis hid some unacknowledged affinities.

His insistence that the struggle against fascism required learning to mourn rather than deny the transience of all things sounded surprisingly like Freud's own thinking.

At the height of the first World War, Sigmund Freud published an essay titled "On Transience," in which he described a psychological reaction he called a "revolt . . . against mourning." Trenches and aerial bombings and poison gas had revealed to all of Europe the fragility and transience of their beloved Western civilization. "We cannot be surprised," Freud wrote, "that our libido, thus bereft of so many of its objects, has clung with all the greater intensity to what is left to us, that our love of country, our affection for those nearest us and our pride in what is common to us have suddenly grown stronger."[4] In the wake of the war, when the frailty and transience of the West was laid bare, people would cling with even more intensity to love of country and affection for those nearest at the expense of all others. The fascist movements rising from the rubble and driving Europe back into war, those awful desperate attempts to preserve forever nation and race, were in Freud's clouded foresight a continent-wide refusal

4. Sigmund Freud, "On Transience," in *On the History of the Psycho-Analytic Movement: Papers on Metapsychology, and Other Works*, trans. James Strachey; The Standard Edition of the Complete Psychological Works of Sigmund Freud 14 (London: Hogarth Press, 1957), 305–7.

to accept the transience of Western civilization—one great revolt against mourning.

For Freud as for Bonhoeffer, the revolt against mourning the loss of some arrangement of culture and power we call "our way of life" leads down a spiral of derangement and violence as more and more becomes sacrificeable in the doomed attempt to cling forever to what is left. Resisting the siren song of civilizational self-preservation through force requires the difficult work of mourning a way of life's inevitable passing. And the work of mourning, as Freud describes it, is Janus-faced: just as twilight is the last light as one day passes and the first light as a new day breaks, mourning looks at once to a lost past and a dawning future. It mingles sorrow and hope. Sorrow, because to mourn is to accept that what was loved is gone and its loss is irrevocable. When we mourn we face an irretrievable past, stubbornly refusing to let go of love just because what we loved is lost. But the pain of mourning is also its paradoxical hope. In our very refusal to get over loss, in carrying the pain of loss from one day to the next, the work of mourning is about the future. When we mourn we just as stubbornly hold fast to a faith that love has a future after loss. To mourn is to let go of what we love while clinging fiercely to love itself, to let love's transforming power make us different from what we have been. Thus for Freud implicitly, and for Bonhoeffer explicitly, the work of mourning works against the will to exclude or eliminate what is different so as to preserve a fantasy of everlasting sameness. If the politics of fascism, with its violent grasping after permanence and power, is animated by a revolt against mourning, resistance must entail learning to mourn.

ॐ

Today we are living through another great revolt against mourning. Climate collapse, accelerating migration, dwindling church attendance, and the decline of Western global hegemony are bringing an end to a familiar Western Christian civilization. The Christian West is dying, a new world is being born, and morbid symptoms flourish.[5]

One particularly morbid symptom has stuck with me for years. In the fall of 2018, a group of about 160 people gathered in San Pedro Sula, Honduras, and began walking north. After over a century of colonial rule, US military intervention to prop up the banana trade, and CIA-backed far-right terror, the already rav-

---

5. Throughout this book, I use the designator "the West"—as in "the Christian West" or "Western civilization"—with the sense given it by Édouard Glissant: "The West is not in the West," Glissant writes. "It is a project, not a place." See Édouard Glissant, *Caribbean Discourse: Selected Essays*, trans. J. Michael Dash (Charlottesville: University Press of Virginia, 1999), 2 n. 1.

aged land was withering under a warming climate. Drought, famine, catastrophic floods, disease, poverty, unemployment, and political instability had made home unlivable. So the group left everything they knew and walked north.[6] As they walked, others for whom home had become a wasteland joined them. Their ranks swelled to over six thousand. In the United States, this so-called migrant caravan became a media spectacle, with outlets like Fox News airing nearly constant coverage of what they began to call an "invasion."

The conservative Christian writer Rod Dreher, author of the influential 2017 book *The Benedict Option*, captured the mood in a series of articles on what he called "the migrant horde." What upset Dreher was not so much the "invaders" themselves but the prospect of cultural replacement they signified. His articles brought together Central American migration to the United States, North African and Middle Eastern migration to Europe, and declining birthrates across countries with white majorities to warn of an all-encompassing threat to "Christian civilization." Taking stock of this threat,

6. Stephanie Leutert, "How Climate Change Is Affecting Rural Honduras and Pushing People North," *Washington Post*, October 28, 2021, https://www.washingtonpost.com/news/global-opinions/wp/2018/11/06/how-climate-change-is-affecting-rural-honduras-and-pushing-people-north/.

Dreher asked his readers: "When, if ever, would lethal force be morally justified against unarmed invaders?"[7]

Dreher's question rattles in my mind every time I read a headline about climate change or global migration. What struck me then and still strikes me now is how haunted he was by his own question. How he seemed dragged against his will into asking it. Dreher seemed to know the idea was unthinkable, but his anxiety that some kind of recognizable "Christian civilization" will soon disappear overwhelmed him and made the unthinkable suddenly thinkable.

This anxiety over the decline and death of a familiar arrangement of religion, race, culture, sex, and gender—Dreher called it "Christian civilization," others call it "Western civilization," others "the Christian West"—seems only to be growing. By 2025, the self-preservation of the Christian West had become something of official state policy in the United States. The 2024 Republican Party platform, on which the party swept to power, promised to "keep foreign Christian-hating" immigrants out of America through the "Largest

7. Rod Dreher, "America's Camp of the Saints Problem," *The American Conservative,* October 22, 2018, https://www. theamericanconservative.com/america-camp-of-the-saints-problem-migrant-caravan/.

Deportation Program in American History."[8] At an inauguration event celebrating the Republican Party's 2024 victory, the billionaire Elon Musk celebrated the party's success by throwing a Nazi salute and crowing that "the future of civilization is secured."[9] The message was clear: by accelerating the violence of the state, the Christian West would be saved.

Rod Dreher's question about when it will become justified to kill "unarmed invaders" has stuck with me because it felt like a foretaste of what is coming as the climate continues to degrade and nationalist forces encircle what resources remain. The scholar Tad Delay has called our historical moment "the start of the greatest migration there ever has been or ever will be."[10] Accelerating climate collapse is making whole swaths of the globe uninhabitable, and the coming decades will only see greater waves of people making the arduous journey to what temperate zones remain. At the same time, resources in the Global North will dwindle.

8. "2024 Republican Party Platform," The American Presidency Project, July 8, 2024, https://www.presidency.ucsb.edu/documents/2024-republican-party-platform.

9. Martin Pengelly, "Elon Musk Appears to Make Back-to-Back Fascist Salutes at Inauguration Rally," *The Guardian*, January 20, 2025, sec. Technology, https://www.theguardian.com/technology/2025/jan/20/trump-elon-musk-salute.

10. Tad DeLay, *Future of Denial: The Ideologies of Climate Change* (New York: Verso, 2024), 28.

As weather patterns become unpredictable and sources of fuel, water, and food deplete, those of us living in Europe and North America will feel we have too little to go around; yet more and more people will arrive. We will be—we are being—asked to share what we feel we do not have. Dreher's question will only come to feel more tempting: will we kill to preserve the Christian West? We have to gather the strength now, in what are the most prosperous and comfortable years we will see for a long time, to answer: no.

❧

This book makes a theological argument against the self-preservation of the Christian West. The priest and scholar Tomáš Halík calls our historical moment "the afternoon of Christianity," but if we narrow our focus to the once-dominant forms of Christianity in Europe and North America, the hour is far later than that.[11] We are in the twilight of the Christian West, as its last lights fade and wholly new lights dawn. Carrying forward Bonhoeffer's call for a Christianity that might mourn its own disappearance as well as his hope that faith might be born anew through this work of mourn-

11. Tomáš Halík, *The Afternoon of Christianity: The Courage to Change*, trans. Gerald Turner (Notre Dame: University of Notre Dame Press, 2024).

ing, this book offers a theology of mourning for a twilit Christianity. Anxieties around cultural decline, disappearance, and replacement, and above all anxiety about the end of Christianity (no matter where on the political spectrum these anxieties surface) are, I will argue, theologically mistaken. Instead of fighting tooth and nail to preserve the last lights of Christendom, we as Christians are called to stand in solidarity with those outside it, even and especially when doing so means the transformation and loss of whatever we might understand as a Christian way of life.

Our task as Christians is not to preserve a given form of Christianity, no matter how beloved that form may be, but to hold it loosely, love it in its passing, and remain open to what new loves may arise in its wake. When we beat back those from different places, of different faiths, living differently gendered lives, all in the name of defending the territory of a properly "Christian" form of life, we lose the very thing we claim to be clinging onto. Transience, loss, "replacement"—these are not threats to a Christian way of life. They are that way of life itself. Our watchword is the angel's words at the empty tomb: "He is not here; he has gone to Galilee." Faith is founded in loss, yet a loss opening out onto a future in which love yet remains possible. This work of reckoning loss and living on in the absence of what we love is the work of mourning. Against the global rise of far-right white nationalisms, movements that present their violence as the only means of preserving a familiar Western Christian culture, this book offers a theology of mourning.

⟡

To mourn is to acknowledge that what is lost was loved. Obscene as I find calls to preserve "Christian civilization" through force, I do understand the grief behind them. I was born and raised in the Episcopal Church, a denomination that, like most others in Europe and North America, is dying. I know what it's like to go to coffee hour after service and hear from the old-timers how noisy families used to pack the upper pews—and to see those pews now used for storage. Like those so anxious about the end of the Christian West, I love the Christian form of life I grew up in and that my parents and my grandparents grew up in, and I grieve its loss. Of course my grief is ambivalent. I recognize that for many, the end of the Christian West is the beginning of a real chance to live. Western Christianity has been, for most people in most places, a Procrustean bed in which countless lives have been mangled and shrunken and forced to conform or cast aside if they would not. The Japanese Catholic novelist Shusaku Endo famously called Christianity an ill-fitting and unbecoming suit, and as its tatters fall away many find it easier to breathe.[12] But I'm not one of them. The suit has fit me fairly well. I will miss it when it's gone. And if you're reading this, I'm guessing on some level you grieve its passing, too.

In the Twilight of the Christian West is written for those who, like me, and however ambivalently, are grieving the loss of the Christian West. It aims to equip us with the means to resist hollow calls to preserve Christianity or Western Civilization through force— calls that will only sound more reasonable and feel more tempting in the coming years—and instead to faithfully mourn its passing.

Over three sections, this book will lay the theological foundation for a politics of resistance to far-right calls to defend the Christian West. It will do so by reframing Christian life as a ceaseless work of mourning. Each section will focus on a different fundamental aspect of Christian belief and practice—creation, the Trinity, Eucharist, and resurrection—exploring how each drives us to reckon the inevitability and irrevocability of loss while moving into an unknown and transforming future.

We will move backward and forward in Christian history, from medieval saints to modern mystics to

12. Jewel Spears Brooker, "In Memoriam: Shusaku Endo," *Christianity & Literature* 48, no. 2 (1999): 141–44.

scattered communities of women gathered in the grave-yards of Palestine in the years just after Jesus's death, in order to trace a Christian tradition very different from that touted by so-called traditionalists and defenders of the faith. This alternate tradition is one in which Christian faith is not some venerable arrangement of power and culture that needs to be preserved from loss and change but is instead a way of living with the fact that nothing can be preserved, that everything—including Christianity—is consigned to loss, that mourning and loss and absence structure our relationships to God and to one another, that to live and to love is always to lose.

॰

Two months after Bonhoeffer's baptism sermon was smuggled out of Tegel prison, the assassination plan was set in motion. Adolf Hitler himself had called a military conference to be held in the gargantuan bunker called the Wolf's Lair on July 20. A few minutes into the meeting, Colonel Claus von Stauffenberg excused himself to the washroom. A few minutes after that, the briefcase he left beside his chair exploded, killing a stenographer but merely singeing the leg of Hitler's pants. The Gestapo investigation into the plot took nearly a year, until on April 4, 1945, the diary of a conspiracist was discovered. Bonhoeffer's brother-in-law Hans von Dohnányi, delirious in his prison cell, having infecting himself with a smuggled handkerchief laced with scarlet fever to avoid interrogation, scrawled a secret message: "They have everything."[13] The diary contained names, even Bonhoeffer's, and though his role in the plot was so minor as to almost nothing at all, the name was enough. Four days later he was transferred to the Flossenbürg concentration camp and executed under the supervision of the sadistic camp doctor Hermann Fischer-Hüllstrung, who liked to cut down the hanged just before they died so they could be revived and hanged again and again.[14] Bonhoeffer died on April 9, one of thousands hastily murdered by the panicking guards as the Americans and Soviets encircled the camp. Two weeks later Flossenbürg was liberated.

Bonhoeffer's call for a Christianity that would have the strength to mourn itself comes down to us only in phrases and fragments, scattered pieces waiting to be picked up and stitched together. This book is an attempt to carry his call forward into the twilight of the Christian West, as Christians are once more tempted to join authoritarian political movements to preserve their communities from disappearance.

13. Bonhoeffer, *Letters and Papers from Prison*, 703.
14. Ferdinand Schlingensiepen, *Dietrich Bonhoeffer, 1906– 1945: Martyr, Thinker, Man of Resistance* (New York: T&T Clark, 2010), 406 n. 8.

Bonhoeffer's friend and teacher Karl Barth warned that fascism was not some external force threatening to corrupt Christianity from without, but was itself born from Christianity; fascism was, Barth insisted, a twisted branch of Christian theology. A mere political or military defeat of fascism, he predicted in 1934, wouldn't be the end of fascism.[15] Fascism had to be defeated *theologically*; Christians had to "take hold of the roots of the malady in our Church," or else it was only a matter of time before something like fascism rose again.[16]

Less than a century later, something like fascism is surely rising again. And once again we must take hold of the roots of the malady and tear them out. In the 1930s, Bonhoeffer went further than anyone in this work, but he was killed before he could clearly set out his theology of mourning. It's up to us to pick up the pieces he left behind.

15. Karl Barth, "No! Answer to Emil Brunner," in *Natural Theology: Comprising "Nature and Grace" by Professor Dr. Emil Brunner and the Reply "No!" by Dr. Karl Barth*, trans. Peter Fraenkel (London: Centenary Press, 1946), 65–128, 112.

16. Karl Barth, *The German Church Conflict*, ed. T.H.L. Parker (Richmond, VA: John Knox Press, 1965), 20.

PART I

Absent Presence

Berlin, 1933

Professor Bonhoeffer kept his head down as he crossed the street onto campus. He had long fantasized about being a theology professor: the echo of shuffling papers in an empty lecture hall, the little jolt of stage fright before the students filed in, shaking off sleep and diving into those thorny ancient questions. It was all he ever wanted. For the first three lectures it had been possible to trick himself, at least while some part of his mind remained asleep, that this was his life. Lecturer in systematic theology at Friedrich Wilhelm University. Living the dream.

He winced. Just three days ago he had checked out some books from the university library and went home for a quiet evening of study. Hours later that same library was raided by the German Student Union. Students (My students? *For three sleepless nights he lay with eyes bolted to the ceiling.* My students? My students?) *had carried off tens of thousands of books to the center of Berlin. There they threw them on a pile of documents looted the week prior from Magnus Hirschfeld's Institute for Sexual Science—once the groundbreaking center for gay and trans health care and activism, now a wreck of broken glass and overturned desks. The mood was festive as Minister of Propaganda Joseph Goebbels led the students in chants: "Against the soul-shredding overestimation of instinctual life! For the nobility of the human soul! I consign the writings of Sigmund Freud to the flames!" Bonhoeffer clutched his own books a bit tighter to his chest as he walked past the smoldering embers and ducked into the lecture hall.*

For the next twelve weeks, Bonhoeffer would lecture on Christology. He'd give his final lecture on July 22, the day before the national church elections, when parishes all across Germany would choose their representatives in the provincial synods. The competing factions were the Nazi-aligned German Christians on one side, and on the other the Confessing Church, which aimed to preserve some meager scrap of church independence. The parishes would choose the Nazis.

The German Christians would go on to win the July 23 elections in a landslide. But for now it was still May, and the fate of Christianity in Germany was still up in the air. Bonhoeffer smiled bitterly as he shuffled his papers. Up in the air? *He glanced quickly at each student as they filed in one by one* (Was it you?)*, sickened at his own mistrust. Some looked as sick as he did. Some looked triumphant.*

It hadn't even begun and it was already over. Professor Bonhoeffer cleared his throat and began his lecture.

෨

As a young doctoral student, Bonhoeffer had aimed to unite theology with sociology in a book on the theological significance of the church. His 1927 dissertation built off of Paul's claim that the church is the body of Christ by coining a curious formula: *Christus als Gemeinde existierend,* "Christ existing as community." His argument, chiseled in the granitelike prose of a German theology dissertation, was as simple as it was radical. Christ does not exist beyond or above Christian communities, as if churches merely "represented" Christ or he represented them. Instead, Christ *is* the community. "The church is the presence of Christ in the same way that Christ is the presence of God," wrote the young Bonhoeffer. "The New Testament knows a form of revelation, 'Christ existing as community.'"[1]

When a community member gets up and reads Scripture in a shaky, stumbling voice, that is how Christ speaks his word. When we confess our sins and

1. Dietrich Bonhoeffer, *Sanctorum Communio: A Theological Study of the Sociology of the Church,* ed. Clifford J. Green and Joachim von Soosten; trans. Reinhard Krauss and Nancy Lukens; Dietrich Bonhoeffer Works 1 (Minneapolis: Fortress Press, 1998), 87.

the community pronounces us forgiven, that is how Christ pronounces his forgiveness. We meet Christ in the church, as the church. Of course, every church community is made up of sinners. But that too is revelation; that too is how Christ exists for us. The church is at the same time *sanctorum communio*, the communion of saints, and *peccatorum communio*, the communion of sinners. Every church is at once Christ's way of being in the world and an all-too-human gathering of sinful people. It's only by being *both* that the church truly reveals to us the incarnate God who is at once human and divine.

So wrote Bonhoeffer in 1927. But now it was 1933. The church as "communion of sinners" was curdling into something else. Soon members of Jewish descent would be expelled. The altars would be draped in swastikas. Prayers of thanksgiving would be bleated out for the "courage" of soldiers lining up Jewish families in front of pits and shooting them in the back. Already churches all over Germany were tearing themselves apart in an absurd "debate" over whether racial segregation could be imposed by the government or whether, as the Confessing Church argued, parishes were more than capable of racially segregating themselves. As Bonhoeffer would claim a year later, 1933 brought an end to the church in Germany. Yet he never let go of the idea that Christian community is how Christ exists in the world. How to square that circle? With every Christian community around him drowning itself in blood and shrieking for more, one question seared his mind like a hot iron: *Who* is this Christ whom the church must be?

Christ, Bonhoeffer told his students in the summer of 1933, is the center of human existence. Yet this center is a strange center, because Christ himself is not the center of his own existence. "The being of Christ's person is essentially relatedness to me. His being-Christ is his being-for-me. . . . The very core of his person is *pro-me*."[2] There is no Christ-in-himself, because Christ is essentially the one who is for others. His existence is entirely given over to those different from himself. This and this alone is Christ's divinity. To say that Jesus is God incarnate is not to say that he is a human with some extra God-ness attached, that he is somehow more or better than any of the rest of us, but to say that he is the one person who exists wholly and only for others—because God just is this perfect gift of self.

In the most provocative moment in the Christology lectures, Bonhoeffer told his students, "If we are to describe Jesus as God, we would not speak of his being all-powerful or all-knowing; we would speak of his birth in a manger and of his cross. There is no 'divine

2. Dietrich Bonhoeffer, *Berlin, 1932–1933*, ed. Larry L. Rasmussen; trans. Isabel Best and David Higgins; Dietrich Bonhoeffer Works 12 (Minneapolis: Fortress Press, 2009), 314.

nature' as all-powerful and ever-present."[3] Manger and cross most perfectly reveal Jesus's divinity because they are moments when he is wholly surrendered into the hands of others: a helpless infant taken up and swaddled by Mary, a lifeless corpse taken up and wrapped in linen by his friends. This is who Jesus is: the one who has no self to preserve, whose existence is at every moment given away.

At the end of his life, Bonhoeffer called on Western Christianity to renounce self-preservation and embrace transformation at the hands of its others. This call, issuing from a baptism sermon that was also an elegy for Christendom, combined his Christology of dispossession with his earlier insistence that Christ exists as community. If Christian community really is Christ's being in the world, and if *who Christ is* is the one who exists not for himself but entirely for others, then Christian communities are paradoxically only *Christian* communities when they too renounce themselves and live wholly for others, even unto their death as Christian communities.

This means a Christian community that fights to preserve itself would be a logical contradiction. Jesus had no self to preserve; his existence is utterly for-others. That churches exist at all testifies to Jesus's will-

3. Bonhoeffer, *Berlin*, 341.

ingness to be "replaced" by the communities that arise
in the wake of his departure. If those communities are
truly to be Christ in the world, they can do so only by
echoing his self-renunciation and giving up their own
being for the sake of others. The church is what it is
only when it opens itself to being replaced by what it
is not. And so, just before his own death, Bonhoeffer
urged Western Christianity to risk everything, even its
own existence, in acts of preserving others from harm.

Should those acts result in the total disappearance
of any familiar form of Christianity, so be it. Such self-
effacement for the sake of the other was what Christianity was all about in the first place. "Our relationship to
God," Bonhoeffer wrote, "is no 'religious' relationship to
some highest, most powerful, and best being imaginable—that is no genuine transcendence." Genuine transcendence, salvation in the truest sense of becoming
like God, is "liberation from self," the transcending of
isolated selfhood in transformative relationships with
others. "Our relationship to God is a new life in 'being
there for others,'" the being-for-others that is God's
own being.[4] It is in ceding whatever "space" Christian
community might have to strange and unfamiliar others that we become what we are, that we are formed to

4. Bonhoeffer, *Letters and Papers from Prison*, 501.

the form of the One whose very being is ceding space for others.

༐

Bonhoeffer's plea for Christianity in the West to renounce self-preservation and embrace the transformations that come with living fully for others has largely gone unheard in the nearly one hundred years since his death. But the specific phenomena he noted as contributing to Western Christianity's disastrous pursuit of self-preservation at all costs are now only compounding. Church membership is declining; the cultural influence of Christianity is fading; and accelerating migration patterns due to the collapse of the climate are bringing ever more strangers to the gates of what were once decidedly white Christian societies. It is past time to push Christianity in the West beyond self-preservation, to imagine new ways of living that Bonhoeffer cryptically called "religionless Christianity." Where he turned to Christology and ecclesiology (the study of the church), this section looks to theologies of creation and the Trinity.

Each chapter of this section focuses on a different moment in twentieth-century theology, with an eye to the centrality of mourning in each. Doing so gives a theological foundation from which we can better respond to the most important political question of our lifetimes:

as the climate crisis continues to accelerate and habitable zones around the world become uninhabitable, how will those of us who live in relatively prosperous societies respond to those fleeing their homes and arriving at our doors? If Tad Delay is correct that we are living at the start of the single greatest period of human migration there ever has or ever will be, then he is also right that we need to learn now, when the world is as stable as it is going to be for a long time, how to respond to the profound and permanent changes such migration will entail. The global right correctly understands that a society that cedes space for climate refugees and stands in solidarity with them would be a society transformed—whatever it had been would be lost, and something new would begin. But the right presents this loss as a catastrophe to be prevented at all costs. The entrenching regime of border walls and climate apartheid is a great revolt against mourning, an attempt to preserve "our way of life" from being "replaced" by outsiders. If instead we begin with Bonhoeffer's call for Christians to mourn the loss of the familiar rather than fighting to prevent its loss, these attempts at civilizational self-preservation start to look blasphemous. This section carries forward Bonhoeffer's theology of mourning by looking at how some of his contemporaries reimagined traditional theological doctrines of creation and the Trinity as themselves structured by mourning.

30   *In the Twilight of the Christian West*

In the first chapter, we'll look at Simone Weil's retelling of the creation story. According to Weil, God created the world not through an act of power but through an act of withdrawal. In the beginning, God stepped back, and in the void where God once was creation arose. The love between God and the world is thus a mourning love, as God forever maintains this estrangement from creation so as to love the world in all its difference from God. Weil's mournful creation theology powerfully rebukes present-day fearmongering about "the Great Replacement," or the dissolution of the Christian West at the hands of foreigners and outsiders. If the very act by which God created the world is an act of making room and letting be, then what gets demonized today as "replacement" is in fact how we live out God's love in the world.

In the second chapter, we'll turn to the trinitarian theology of the Swiss physician and mystic Adrienne von Speyr and her confessor and scribe, Hans Urs von Balthasar. Their theology of the Trinity focuses on the difference and distance between God the Father and God the Son, the space that holds them apart and yet at the same time makes possible any love between them. Trinitarian theology is for them a theology of mourning, as they see the infinite separation between Father and Son on Holy Saturday as stretching God's love to an infinite distance. With reference to the Caribbean philosopher Édouard Glissant, I draw out from their theology a radical antifascist politics that they were unable to see themselves. Von Speyr and von Balthasar's trinitarian affirmation of difference and distance can ground a political response to our age of accelerating climate migration, one beyond both liberalism's superficial "welcome culture" and the right's politics of global segregation. Weil, von Speyr, and von Balthasar form the bedrock of a theology of mourning that the remainder of this book will explore.

CHAPTER 1

Simone Weil
Creation as Replacement

A specter is haunting the Christian West—the specter of replacement. Church attendance across Europe and North America is declining rapidly. Gender roles cemented during the postwar years are giving way to new expressions of sex, gender, and the family. Climate collapse and political instability in increasingly arid zones are driving more and more migration toward the temperate North. Familiar cultural forms whither and disappear as new ones arise. Everywhere strange people, strange languages, strange religions. Whatever the Christian West may have been, it is contracting, and a new world is expanding to fill the void.

Some rage against the dying of the light, decrying the "Great Replacement" of a familiar Western Christian culture by unfamiliar outsiders. There's a kind of mathematical logic to this fear: to cede space to those who

32

are different, to live alongside others and be changed by that living, is a loss for "us" and a gain for "them." A church is torn down and a mosque replaces it; the sounds of English on the street are replaced by Spanish or Arabic; familiar gender relations are replaced by new norms and unfamiliar pronouns. Subtract from one side and add to another. The opponents of the so-called Great Replacement present themselves as preserving Western Christian civilization from this kind of subtraction: by preventing those without from gaining, they prevent those within from losing.

But they have their math backward. In the creation theology of the philosopher, mystic, and amateur mathematician Simone Weil, God creates the world through an act of subtraction, diminishing Godself and ceding space so that which is not God can arise. Our task, as Weil describes it, is to echo this self-subtracting love, ceaselessly withdrawing in order that others can fill the space we have ceded. In that way, her creation theology is a powerful rejoinder to those anxious about the "replacement" of the Christian West. With her, we have the foundation of a twilit Christianity that might faithfully mourn its own diminishment, seeing its own loss as truer gain.

☙

In the beginning God was replaced. So writes Simone Weil, with a logic no less mathematical than that of the opponents of "replacement." Infinite God plus finite creation equals something less than infinite God alone. Creation is not addition but subtraction. "On God's part," she writes, "creation is not an act of self-expansion but of restraint and renunciation."[1] While Christian theologians often narrate creation as an act of power or an overflowing of God's fullness, Weil sees that the existence of finite creation requires the lessening of God's infinitude. In creating the world, God stepped back and made room, freeing up space for creation to arise. And the ongoingness of the world requires not God's continual intervention but God's continual restraint, a continual consent on God's part to surrender mastery and allow that which is not God to remain in all its not-Godness. The world as "less than God," so to speak, must not be "filled up" by divine infinitude, as then it would cease to exist as world, as something other than God.

God "stays far away from us, because if He approached He would cause us to disappear," Weil writes.[2] And so God loves the world at a distance, "per-

1. Simone Weil, *Waiting for God*, trans. Emma Craufurd (New York: Routledge, 2021), 96.
2. Simone Weil, *First and Last Notebooks: Supernatural Knowledge*, trans. Richard Rees (Eugene, OR: Wipf & Stock Publishers, 2015), 142.

mitting a part of being to be other than God."[3] Weil
consistently narrates creation with this kind of passive
language: permission, consent, acceptance, surrender, effacement. Viewing creation as an act of letting
go and letting be, Weil inscribes loss in the very fabric
of the world: in the beginning God loses something of
Godself; God becomes less so that which is not God
can become more, and God forever preserves the difference between God and world, forever loving us at a
distance.

This act of stepping back and letting be simply is
what God is. Thomas Aquinas describes God as "pure
act," that "potentiality is not in God, but only active
power."[4] In other words, God does not exist independently of God's acts, as if God were some being floating
around in the great beyond who one day decided to act.
God is what God does. And what God does is love.

Weil, though no fan of Aquinas, takes his theological
logic and runs with it. The loving act that God only is,
for her, is one continuous movement of self-effacement.
"Creation, Passion, Eucharist," she writes, "—always

3. Simone Weil, *Intimations of Christianity among the
Ancient Greeks*, trans. Elizabeth Chase Geissbuhler (New York:
Routledge, 1998), 193.
4. Thomas Aquinas, *Summa Theologica*, trans. Fathers of
the English Dominican Province (Notre Dame, IN: Christian
Classics, 2000), Ia, q. 25, ad. 1.

the same movement of withdrawal. This movement is love."[5] God is none other than this movement of self-loss, this eternal being-for-others, an infinite love lived out as making room for others, as allowing what is God to be replaced by what is not.

Already we can see how any anxiety about cultural "replacement," any desire to preserve the glory of a "Christian civilization," or even the more humble and understandable desire to preserve a beloved form of Christian life from being forever lost misses something essential. So too the work of making Christians of those who are not—through missions and evangelizing—cuts against the grain of God's self-effacing act. Cardinal Jean-Paul Vesco said something similar when he was made archbishop of Algiers in 2022, claiming that a true evangelism worthy of the name would involve not conversion but simply attending to the needs of others in all their difference.[6] His understanding of evangelism sounds like what Weil calls "attention," those acts that echo God's creative self-loss. "To accept that [others] should be other than the creatures of our imagination is

---

5. Weil, *First and Last Notebooks*, 81.

6. Laurence D'Hondt, "'Il faut nous défaire de l'idée que nous devons évangéliser,'" Portail catholique suisse, February 6, 2022, https://www.cath.ch/newsf/il-faut-nous-defaire-de-lidee-que-nous-devons-evangeliser/.

to imitate the renunciation of God," Weil says of attention; "to accept simply that they should *be*."[7]

Cardinal Vesco, for his principled refusal to convert others to Christianity, was roundly denounced in publications like the *European Conservative*, accused of abetting the replacement of white Europeans who must now "bow to the massive influx of migrants who pour into their territory every year."[8] But the cardinal, like Weil, follows a different mathematical logic than the defenders of the Christian West. God's creative act, the very condition of our existing at all, is God's making room for what is not God and loving it in all its difference from God. Any time we refuse to make room for others, any time we build walls around the familiar to protect it from the presence of the unfamiliar, any time we demand those who are different assimilate and become more like us—any time, that is, that we use force to preserve "us" from the corroding presence of "them"—we refuse to follow the love in which and for which we were created.

༒

7. Simone Weil, *The Notebooks of Simone Weil*, trans. Arthur Wills (New York: Routledge, 2004), 200.

8. Hélène de Lauzun, "A Catalogue of New Sins: A Catholic Self-Criticism Session?" *The European Conservative,* October 7, 2024, https://europeanconservative.com/articles/commentary/a-catalogue-of-new-sins-a-catholic-self-criticism-session/.

Simone Weil wrote her essays on creation while living in Marseilles, having fled south with her family when the Nazis conquered Paris in 1940. Germany divided France into a northern "occupied zone" and a southern "free zone." That the south was called "free" was a cruel joke. All it meant was that the government head-quartered in the resort town of Vichy was not directly administered by the Nazi occupation. Free to govern the south, the Vichy government imposed its own authoritarian rule and draconian anti-Jewish laws.

Weil, born into a Jewish family, cultivated her own ambivalent and idiosyncratic religious sensibilities. She was allergic to any collective identity (French, communist, Jew, woman) and cobbled together what she considered religious truth wherever she found it: ancient Greek mystery religions, the wisdom literature of the Hebrew Bible, African American spirituals, Kabbalah, Christian mysticism, the Egyptian Book of the Dead. She was uncategorizable.

But fascists fear ambivalence and ambiguity. In his analysis of far-right literature in 1930s Germany, Klaus Theweleit sums up the fascist rage for rigidity and order: "Nothing is to be permitted to flow. . . . Death to all that flows."[9] Simone Weil flowed. So the law tried

9. Klaus Theweleit, *Male Fantasies, Volume 1: Women, Floods, Bodies, Histories*, trans. Stephen Conway (Minneapolis: University of Minnesota Press, 1987), 230.

to pin her down. She was barred from teaching and eventually begged friends and acquaintances for a job as an agricultural laborer. In the meantime, she distributed Catholic anti-Nazi literature on the streets of Marseilles. Though drawn to Christianity, she refused to be baptized, an act of solidarity with the outsiders and heretics and Jews whom Christians have over the centuries declared damned. She continued to flow, always beyond definition, ever slipping from the fascists' fingers.

These experiences of being a Jew, a woman, a refugee—exiled, shoved to the margins, harassed by the police; always in fear of torture, deportation, execution—opened Weil's eyes to the *sine qua non* of her theology: God does not dominate. "He is withdrawn from all contact with might."[10] Earlier I said that Weil's reasoning behind her theology of withdrawal and divine absence is mathematical, but even more than that, it's moral.

Justice, for Weil, is when someone who is stronger behaves toward the weaker *as if* they were of equal strength. She dreamed of one day carving a statue of Justice: a woman exhausted, blindfolded, hands chained behind her back, stumbling toward a scale

10. Weil, *Intimations of Christianity*, 120.

whose unequal arms held two equal weights.[11] Justice involves sizing up real differences in power and then acting exactly as if those differences did not exist. "Exactly, in every respect, including the slightest details of accent and attitude."[12]

A Jewish refugee wandering through a Christian Europe consuming itself in antisemitic madness, Weil knew the brutality of naked domination as well as the subtle indignities of condescension, pity, and self-righteous charity. While in Marseilles, she befriended Indo-Chinese laborers the French government had conscripted from the colonies to manufacture weapons. And when the police routinely rounded them up, she attended their court trials.[13] She wrote of her horror watching migrants "[standing] broken down by guilt, affliction and fear, stammering before judges who are not listening and who interrupt [them] in tones of ostentatious refinement."[14] From her horror at the ways migrants were humiliated and dehumanized by the affected loftiness of the law, Weil spun her

11. The statue is discussed in Jacqueline Rose, *The Plague* (London: Fitzcarraldo Editions, 2023), 95.

12. Weil, *Waiting for God*, 94.

13. Benjamin P. Davis, *Simone Weil's Political Philosophy: Field Notes from the Margins* (Lanham, MD: Rowman & Littlefield, 2023), 53.

14. Weil, *Waiting for God*, 105.

radical notion of justice as the refusal of any kind of domination.

Christianity, Weil lamented, too often imagines God primarily as dominating. Her ambivalence toward Christianity deepened with her experience of exile. She fled with her parents from France to New York, then left them behind and traveled alone to London in a desperate and failed attempt to get back to France to join the Resistance. While in London, she wrote a devastating critique of Christian theology's long history of imagining God in terms of power, accusing such theology of paving the road to fascism. "Let us imagine some great Roman master owning vast estates and numerous slaves," she says. "Then let us expand the estate to the dimensions of the universe. That is the conception of God that in fact dominates a portion of Christianity, and which has perhaps defiled more or less all of Christianity, except the mystics."[15]

When Christian theology speaks of God's greatness, often it speaks only of power. God is great, we often say, because God is all-powerful, majestic, the king of kings and lord of lords. But this idea that greatness has to do with the exercise of power, Weil cuttingly points out, is

15. Simone Weil, *The Need for Roots: Prelude to a Declaration of Duties Towards Mankind*, trans. Arthur Wills (New York: Routledge, 2002), 276.

"the very one which has inspired Hitler's whole life."[16] Hitler, too, thought that it is great to be master over others, great to rule, great to be ensconced in the pomp and circumstance of sovereignty.

Weil describes the task of theology as to effect "such a total transformation of the meaning attached to greatness that [Hitler] should thereby be excluded from it."[17] This is what "the mystics"—her cryptic name for the minor chord humming through the history of theology—describe: an alternate vision of God's greatness. For Weil, this other greatness, what she calls "true greatness," is not the exercise of force but its absolute and uncompromising refusal.

༼

It's here, in this idea of God's perfect refusal of force, that we can see how mourning forms the bedrock of Weil's theology. The writer Susan Taubes once noted that Weil's theology centers on a "negative theodicy."[18] *Theodicy* is the name for the riddle of evil: If God is all-powerful and all-good, why is there evil? Why is the world so weary with suffering? Various answers have

---

16. Weil, *The Need for Roots,* 217.
17. Weil, *The Need for Roots,* 224.
18. Susan Taubes, "The Absent God: A Study of Simone Weil" (PhD diss., Harvard University, 1956), 302.

been given. Perhaps God is all-powerful but not all-good, some kind of cosmic torturer. Or perhaps God is all-good but not all-powerful, a kind of well-meaning bumbler. For most of Christian history, most theologians have charted a course through theodicy by appealing to the mystery of divine providence. The world might appear to be chaos, evil might appear everywhere to reign, but there is, as the novelist Marilynn Robinson put it, "a mysterious, benign intention" thrumming through history and shepherding our unruly actions along a foreordained plan.[19]

Weil had no truck with this. Like Ivan Karamazov, she saw the idea that history partakes of a "higher harmony" or moves to some blessed consummation as a selfish strategy to avoid truly seeing the suffering of another person.[20] Providential accounts of history, for her, are ways of soothing our own distress at the sight of another's pain, of saying *It's not as bad as it seems*, or *God has a plan*, and looking away.

For Weil, history has no harmony and follows no plan. The arc of history, in her eyes, bends not toward justice but toward catastrophe. Every step of so-called

19. Marilynne Robinson, *Reading Genesis* (New York: Farrar, Straus and Giroux, 2024), 15.
20. Fyodor Dostoevsky, *The Brothers Karamazov*, trans. Richard Pevear and Larissa Volokhonsky (New York: Farrar, Straus and Giroux, 2002), 245.

progress brings new depths of barbarism. History is, she writes, "a tissue of base and cruel acts," an endless litany of violence.[21] Her watchword is a line from Thucydides supposedly spoken by the Athenian navy before their genocide of the Melian people: "The strong do what they can, and the weak suffer what they must."

Weil saw the world as "completely empty of God," entirely given over to the reign of force.[22] Her theological writings are lacerated by her anguish over God's absence. She saw the purest image of the relationship between God and the world as the moment when Jesus cried from the cross, "My God, my God, why have you forsaken me?," and heard in reply nothing at all. Like Nietzsche's madman, she grieved to her bones the death of God.

And yet she found faith within her mourning. She insisted that the absence of God, the omnipresence of suffering, the seeming omnipotence of evil, and the utter godforsakenness of the world are in fact the surest proofs of God's abiding love.

This might sound absurd, but Weil's logic is as methodical as ever. Evil is the domination of the weak by the strong. When we see gratuitous acts of cruelty and domination, we often cry out to God to step in and

21. Weil, *The Need for Roots*, 229.
22. Weil, *Notebooks*, 424.

stop the evildoers. But if God were to do this, were the heavens to part and the hand of God stretch down and force the masters of war and oppression to cease, this would be yet one more instance of the stronger bending the weaker to their will.

This would not be a rebuke of the dominators but their vindication: the Roman master who imposes his will on his vast estate would differ from God in degree but not in kind. We might protest that the Roman master—or, for that matter, the Gestapo agents who harassed and arrested Weil and whose tortures she constantly feared—dominates for ill and God would dominate for good. But, for Weil, there simply is no such thing as "dominating for good."

God's perfect goodness requires that God always and everywhere refuse domination. This is the "negative theodicy": If God is infinitely powerful as well as infinitely good, and if creation is merely finite, then for God to act upon creation at all would be an act of domination. Therefore God does not act. God's relationship to the world is instead one of passivity: not acting but suffering, not ruling but permitting, not appearing but withdrawing.[23] God relates to the world not as the presence of a divine master but as the absence of a lost love. The godforsakenness of the world, God's agoniz-

23. Weil, *Intimations of Christianity*, 118.

ing absence, is thus for Weil proof that God is both all-powerful and all-good, all-good because refusing ever to exercise that power.

This is why Weil famously claims that "atheism is a purification," because the atheist is more deeply aware of God's absence from the world than the theist.[24] But atheism is only a step on the way. Better still is awareness that the absence of God from the world is itself God's presence, because God is a love that withdraws and allows the world to exist as other than God, however agonizing that difference and distance from God may be.

Weil's gloomy pessimism here opens out onto faith. If God is absent from creation because God lovingly refuses to dominate, and if God *just is* this love that steps back and lets be, then this absence is a strange kind of presence. God's absence from the world is the paradoxical presence of a love lived out as withdrawal and restraint. Her theology of mourning also opens out onto the genuinely joyful insight that the absent presence of God's self-effacing love is encountered in the staggering diversity of creation. If God's love is enacted by letting the world be in all its difference from God, then we meet that love when we open ourselves to the world's proliferating difference.

24. Weil, *Notebooks*, 126.

Thus, for her, it is in mourning God's absence that we are enfolded into the love that God only ever is. "Contact with God is given to us through the sense of absence," she writes. "Compared with this absence, presence becomes more absent than absence."[25] Weil's theological writings are shot through with this interplay of presence and absence, this insistence that God's absence *is* God's presence. When someone we love dies, she writes, "the presence of the dead one is imaginary, but his absence is very real; it is henceforth his manner of appearing."[26] Weil strove to love God with this kind of mourning love, seeing God's absence as in fact God's manner of appearing.

Though the world is infinitely separated from an absent God, "the infinite distance is made of the totality of space and time," meaning "we are nothing other than a point" through which passes God's infinite love.[27] For Weil, it is precisely to those most unlike our conceptions of godliness and greatness and glory we must turn in order to glimpse the God who is known only in what appears to us ungodly and inglorious.

ॐ

25. Weil, *Notebooks*, 240.
26. Weil, *Notebooks*, 28.
27. Weil, *Intimations of Christianity*, 197.

Weil's mournful theology of creation makes nonsense of the fearmongering about "replacement" so prevalent in the twilight of the Christian West. The idea of the "Great Replacement" began on the fringes of the extreme European right but has quickly taken over the political center of Europe and America. The term comes from the French writer and politician Renaud Camus, whose spluttering essays seethe against the indignity of walking down a familiar street and seeing unfamiliar faces, faces "who appear to belong to other shores, other skies, other architectures, other customs." Camus describes immigrants as an inhuman force, like a plague or a tsunami, an "endless tide" of human difference crashing on Christendom's shores "with their families, establishing their progeny here, radically transforming its appearance and that of its streets."[28] With his wounded childlike raving that things should stay exactly as he remembers them forever, Camus reads like a parochial crank. But this crank touched a nerve. Soon his phrase captured a fear tremulating through the remains of the Christian West, and was quickly taken up by pundits around the world. A study in late 2022 showed about a third of Americans, and nearly three quarters of those who voted for Donald Trump,

28. Renaud Camus, *Enemy of the Disaster: Selected Political Writings of Renaud Camus*, ed. Louis Betty and Ethan S. Rundell (Blowing Rock, NC: Vauban Books, 2023), 104, 128.

now believe that immigration is a deliberate strategy by shadowy elites to destroy the nation's identity and take control.[29]

On the global right, particular ire is reserved for the leaders of the Catholic Church. Above all, for Pope Francis, whose papacy focused on compassion for migrants and indigenous peoples afflicted by the climate crisis. Another French writer-politician, Philippe de Villiers, called Francis "the Pope of the Camp of the Saints," referencing travel writer Jean Raspail's racist fable in which subhuman migrant savages invade and destroy Europe.[30] (We'll return to *The Camp of the Saints* in chapter 6.) When Pope Francis opened a 2024 synod by leading the cardinals in praying for forgiveness for sins against "creation, indigenous peoples, and migrants," the *European Conservative* likened it to "Soviet-style self-criticism."[31] Rod Dreher, speaking at the 2024 National Conservatism conference in Brus-

29. Jared Sharpe, "New National UMass Amherst Poll on Issues Finds One-Third of Americans Believe 'Great Replacement' Theory," UMassAmherst.edu, October 25, 2022, https://www.umass.edu/news/article/new-national-umass-amherst-poll-issues-finds-one-third-americans-believe-great.

30. José Pedro Zúquete, "The European Alt-Right's Crusade against Pope Francis," *Church Life Journal,* August 7, 2020, https://churchlifejournal.nd.edu/articles/the-european-alt-rights-crusade-against-pope-francis/.

31. Lauzun, "A Catalogue of New Sins."

sels, denounced the Catholic Church as abetting the European Union in its scheme of "sexual revolution, open borders, and indeed long-term Islamization." The Catholic Church under Pope Francis, he proclaimed, is little more than a corps of "hospice chaplains blessing the euthanasia of European civilization.[32] The point was put most straightforwardly by Charles Cornish-Dale, a former medieval historian turned far-right body-building lifestyle blogger who writes under the pseudonym "Raw Egg Nationalist" and who has appeared as a guest on mainstream conservative programs like *Tucker Carlson Tonight*, Glenn Beck's BlazeTV, and the podcast hosted by evangelical Bonhoeffer biographer Eric Metaxas. In his magazine *Man's World*, Cornish-Dale declared, "The Church doesn't want a revival of Western civilization in any sense we might recognise or desire. The Church wants the Great Replacement."[33]

It's true that many leaders of the Catholic Church, above all Pope Francis, have denounced anti-migrant xenophobia and have organized heroic efforts to wel-

32. Rod Dreher, "Chaplains of Decline: The Church and Post-Christian Europe" (National Conservatism, Brussels, Belgium, April 16, 2024), https://nationalconservatism.org/natcon-brussels-2/presenters/rod-dreher/.
33. Raw Egg Nationalist, "A Vitalist Christianity? Don't Bet on It," *Man's World*, April 21, 2024, https://mansworldmag.online/vitalist-christianity-dont-bet-on-it/.

come refugees and asylum seekers. But shift your perspective from immigration to gender and sexuality, and the fear of a familiar way of life being replaced by the strange habits of threatening outsiders lingers. Pope Francis himself frequently denounced what he called "gender ideology" as an existential threat, comparing it to such destructive evils as colonialism, nuclear weapons, and the Hitler Youth.[34] Francis at times made overtures toward acceptance of transgender people, but his hyperbolic denunciations of "gender ideology" undermined these gestures and in fact helped fuel the rise of the far right in Europe and the United States. As University of Chicago Law School professor Mary Anne Case has shown, the term "gender ideology" emerged from official Catholic Church circles in the 1990s,

---

34. Courtney Mares, "Pope Francis: Gender Ideology Is One of the Most Dangerous Ideological Colonizations Today," Catholic News Agency, accessed March 26, 2025, https://www. catholicnewsagency.com/news/253845/pope-francis-gender-ideology-is-one-of-the-most-dangerous-ideological-coloniza tions-today; Joshua J. McElwee, "Francis Strongly Criticizes Gender Theory, Comparing It to Nuclear Arms," *National Catholic Reporter,* February 13, 2015, https://www.ncronline. org/news/vatican/francis-strongly-criticizes-gender-theory-comparing-it-nuclear-arms; Joshua J. McElwee, "Francis Lambasts International Aid, Suggests Catholics Should Limit Children," *National Catholic Reporter,* January 19, 2015, https:// www.ncronline.org/news/francis-lambasts-international-aid-suggests-catholics-should-limit-children.

culminating in the Pontifical Council for the Family's 2000 statement warning of "the spread of a certain ideology of 'gender'" according to which "being a man or a woman" is culturally constructed.[35] This idea of a nefarious "gender ideology" was quickly picked up by the global right. Scholars like Eva von Redecker, Elżbieta Korolczuk, and Agnieszka Graff have traced how "gender ideology" has become "a 'symbolic glue' linking the programs and discourses of far-right and conservative parties" in Europe and the United States.[36] Francis is often remembered as a counterweight to the

35.   Mary Anne Case, "Trans Formations in the Vatican's War on 'Gender Ideology,'" *Signs: Journal of Women in Culture and Society* 44, no. 3 (March 2019): 639–64, https://doi.org/10.1086/701498; "Family, Marriage and 'de Facto' Unions" (Pontifical Council for the Family, July 26, 2000), https://www.vatican.va/roman_curia/pontifical_councils/family/documents/rc_pc_family_doc_20001109_de-facto-unions_en.html.

36.   Agnieszka Graff and Elżbieta Korolczuk, *Anti-Gender Politics in the Populist Moment* (New York: Routledge, 2022), 799; Eva von Redecker, "*Anti-Genderismus* and Right-Wing Hegemony," *Radical Philosophy* 198 (2016): 2–7. See also Elizabeth S. Corredor, "Unpacking 'Gender Ideology' and the Global Right's Antigender Countermovement," *Signs: Journal of Women in Culture and Society* 44, no. 3 (March 2019): 613–38, https://doi.org/10.1086/701171; S. J. Crasnow, "The Legacy of 'Gender Ideology': Anti-Trans Legislation and Conservative Christianity's Ongoing Influence on U.S. Law," *Religion and Gender* 11, no. 1 (June 23, 2021): 67–71, https://doi.org/10.1163/18785417-01101005.

global right, but his apocalyptic rhetoric about "gender ideology" helped accelerate the fusion of traditional conservatives and the far right across Europe and North America. Lurking underneath both anti-migrant xenophobia and opposition to "gender ideology" lies the fear that a familiar way of life is being replaced.

∾

The specter of replacement stalks the twilight of the Christian West. But Simone Weil's creation theology can exorcize this phantom. What is demonized, explicitly or implicitly, as "replacement"—ceding space for someone quite different from oneself and being transformed by this encounter—is not something from which a "Christian way of life" must be protected. Rather it is, as she reveals, the very substance of the Christian life. Making room for those who are different and letting them be in all their difference is, in her telling of creation, the heart of the Christian story. God withdraws, and that which is not God fills the voided space. We swim with the current of God's creative love not when we forcefully defend a recognizable Christian culture, but when we withdraw in love and make space for the flourishing of those who are different from ourselves.

Weil's theology also makes room for the sorrow we might feel at the passing of beloved cultural forms.

Yet she insists that the loss of any recognizable form of Christianity through which we have come to know God's love is not the loss of that love itself. What our faith was about in the first place, after all, is a God who lets go of Godself and loves the sheer otherness of the world. That our world is rapidly becoming more and more other than what we have known is simply a fuller opportunity to participate in that love.

At the same time, Weil's profound pessimism about history helps make theological sense of the revolt against mourning gripping what remains of the Christian West. For now at least, the forces of reaction are winning. Calls to defend the Christian West are raised and heeded, walls are built, those seen as too different are hounded across borders and back into closets. As climate collapse accelerates and resources dwindle, we should not expect the arc of history to bend toward justice. But neither can we shirk the demand to follow God's self-effacing love and renounce what we imagine "we" have for the sake of another's real need. Weil pushes us to understand these much-needed acts of solidarity, self-renunciation, and, yes, "replacement," as ways of being pulled along into God's mourning love.

CHAPTER 2

Adrienne von Speyr and Hans Urs von Balthasar
Difference, Distance, and the Trinity

On August 27, 2015, Austrian police responded to a call about an abandoned 18-wheeler parked off the side of a highway. A construction worker mowing grass nearby had noticed what looked like blood dripping from the truck's rear doors. The truck had been sitting in the hot sun for over a day. When police opened the doors, they found what they later determined to be the bodies of seventy-one refugees from Syria, Iraq, and Afghanistan. At the time it was impossible to tell. Having suffocated to death, the people in the truck decomposed together to the point where they could be identified only by the objects they left behind.[1]

---

1. Bethany Bell and Nick Thorpe, "Austria's Migrant Disaster: Why Did 71 Die?" BBC News, August 24, 2016, sec. Europe, https://www.bbc.com/news/world-europe-37163217.

A few days later, German Chancellor Angela Merkel visited a refugee camp near Dresden and gave a press conference. The situation facing Germany seemed overwhelming. Syria, Iraq, and Afghanistan, their land devastated by famine and drought accelerated by the climate crisis, their economies and governments decimated by Western military adventures, had descended into chaos. Home was no longer livable. So people took to the sea and took to the roads, heading toward the European countries that had for so long enriched themselves at their expense.

At her press conference, Merkel reframed the so-called migrant crisis as a challenge. "Wir schaffen das," she thundered. We can do this. That year, 2015, saw more asylum seekers in Europe than any year since the second World War. Germany would forever bear the shame of that earlier catastrophe, but this time things could be different. We can do this.

A decade later, Merkel's *Willkommenskultur,* or "welcome culture," has collapsed. The far-right extremist party Alternativ für Deutschland, after distributing campaign literature with images of blond-haired blue-eyed families doing the Nazi salute, put up better numbers in the 2024 elections than they ever had, becoming the first far-right party to win a statewide election since the Nazis. This despite a scandal in which leaders of the AfD met in secret with various neo-Nazis to discuss a "master plan" of constructing a special economic zone in North Africa to which immigrants and "non-assimilated citizens" could be rounded up and deported. Also in attendance at that 2023 meeting were members of Merkel's own party, the Christian Democratic Union.[2]

How could Merkel's welcome culture sit so snugly alongside the genocidal xenophobia of the extreme right? Activist and writer Harsha Walia explained that while the idea of "welcoming immigrants" is nice in the abstract, in concrete terms Germany under Merkel only welcomed immigrants to the extent that they contributed to the economy or assimilated to the culture.[3]

We can see a similar dynamic in the United States. Liberal politicians condemn their opponents' xenophobic language, but their own speeches limit praise to "hard-working" immigrants, grateful and patriotic guests who keep their heads down, work hard, and follow the rules. Like the line from the beloved liberal musical *Hamilton* goes, "Immigrants—we get the job done!"[4] This is what the philosopher Jacques Derrida

2. Linda Mannheim, "The AfD's Secret Plan to Deport Millions from Germany," *The Nation,* January 23, 2024, https://www.thenation.com/article/world/germany-afd-secret-meeting-deportation/.

3. Harsha Walia, *Border and Rule: Global Migration, Capitalism, and the Rise of Racist Nationalism* (Chicago: Haymarket Books, 2021), 122.

4. I'm grateful to Michael Putnam for pointing me to this example.

calls "conditional hospitality": "The host remains the master in the house, the country, the nation, he controls the threshold, he controls the borders, and when he welcomes the guest he wants to keep the mastery."[5]

But hospitality with conditions is not true hospitality. To welcome someone only to the extent that they behave how we wish is not to welcome *this person* in all their unpredictability and indeterminacy, but a figment of our imagination and thus an extension of our own selves. In Germany, as in the United States, when times get hard, immigrants are easy to scapegoat as simply too other to belong. The nation's ills are blamed on them not assimilating or them receiving too much government assistance. "We can do this," but only so long as we remain masters of the house, only so long as all these strangers stop being so strange.

Where liberal "welcome culture" tends to welcome others to the extent that they assimilate and become less other, right-wing politicians across Europe and North America have begun presenting themselves as surprising champions of cultural difference. In their recent book *World of the Right: Radical Conservatism and Global Order*, a team of political scientists track

5. Jacques Derrida, "Hospitality, Justice and Responsibility: A Dialogue with Jacques Derrida," in *Questioning Ethics: Contemporary Debates in Philosophy*, ed. Richard Kearney and Mark Dooley (New York: Routledge, 1999), 65–83, 69.

how what we in the United States tend to reductively call "Christian nationalism" is in fact a profoundly *international* movement. Nationalist groups present themselves as opposing the hegemony of liberal globalism through what the authors call "differentialism: the idea that cultures or civilisations are incommensurably diverse and that none has a claim to validity or virtue."[6] But this claim to defend cultural difference is a mile wide and an inch deep. The right's vision of the world as a diverse patchwork of different cultures serves to legitimize further practices of exclusion and domination. Hondurans shouldn't be forced to assimilate and become hard-working and patriotic Americans, say these self-styled defenders of difference, because they shouldn't be in America at all—they should stay over there, with their own kind, and also they should keep those cheap resources flowing.

Both of these approaches to human difference fail to meet the challenge of the Greatest Migration.[7] Voices on the right say that others are free to be as different as they like, so long as they stay away. Liberal voices say that others are welcome here, so long as they become less

6. Rita Abrahamsen et al., *World of the Right: Radical Conservatism and Global Order* (Cambridge: Cambridge University Press, 2024), 149–50, https://doi.org/10.1017/9781009516075.

7. Tad DeLay, *Future of Denial: The Ideologies of Climate Change* (New York: Verso, 2024).

different. The former want difference without relation (meaning they don't actually want difference); the latter want relation without difference (meaning they don't actually want relation). Both approaches are not only incoherent and violent. They're theologically mistaken.

༄

At the center of Christian theology is a mystery of sameness and difference: God is one God in three persons. The famous icon by Andrei Rublev depicts God as three persons sitting around a table with a dish between them, each surrendering the dish to the others. The love of God, the love that is God, is a love *between* different persons. It's a love in which difference and otherness aren't overcome but preserved, in which separation and distance don't foreclose relation but are the absence across which relation happens. Approaching this mystery from the perspective of a theology of mourning troubles whatever conditions we might want to put on our hospitality in the twilight of the Christian West.

With Weil, we saw how God's absence from the world "here below" is in fact the presence of God's withdrawing love. God loves the world by stepping back and letting be, freeing creation to be what it is and loving it at a distance. And we saw how this makes our relationship to God a mourning in Freud's sense: a longing for one who is absent that then pulls us out of ourselves toward present others whom we might love.

In this chapter, as we look at the trinitarian theology offered by two Swiss theologians from the twentieth century, we'll explore how this mourning love structures not only our love for God and God's love for us, but God's love for Godself. Adrienne von Speyr and Hans Urs von Balthasar together describe the internal life of God as an infinite longing, an infinite mourning stretching between a grieving Father and a dead Son.

Because this infinite grief is God, and because God is love, this absolute separation is at once the deepest intimacy between God and God; the distance between Father and Son is at once the absent presence of the love that ever binds them. Von Speyr and von Balthasar's trinitarian theology of mourning thus reorients our relationship to difference and distance. Instead of being an obstacle to relation, every finite separation between us is nested within the infinite separation between God and God—that is, it is the differences between us that form the absent presence of God's longing love.

Yet von Speyr and von Balthasar remained frustratingly blind to the political demands of their radical theological affirmation of difference. Though they lived right next door to a Germany descending into fascism, they held silent. This chapter reads their radical theology against their lukewarm politics by putting them in conversation with the Caribbean philosopher Édouard Glissant, whose concept of "the right to opacity" can teach us how to live out a trinitarian theology of mourning.

∽

In 1940 in the Swiss city of Basel—where Karl Barth was denouncing fascism as a twisted branch of Christianity—a doctor named Adrienne von Speyr was introduced by mutual friends to a university chaplain named Hans Urs von Balthasar. It was immediately clear to von Balthasar that von Speyr was an extraordinary woman; after all, she was one of the first women in Switzerland to become a physician. She was also, secretly, a mystic. From around the time she met von Balthasar until her death in 1967, von Speyr experienced visions of Jesus's death on the cross and his descent into hell. She drew from these visions spiritual lessons and scriptural commentaries that she dictated to von Balthasar, her confessor and later spiritual director and friend.

Perhaps the most influential Catholic theologian of the last century, von Balthasar incorporated von Speyr's ideas into massive, multivolume works of systematic theology. From their friendship would arise a haunting theology of the Trinity that foregrounds loss and estrangement as the very essence of God's love.

Von Speyr and von Balthasar describe the love between God and world and the love between God and God as infinite mourning, a love that sorrowfully reckons the insuperable void between lover and beloved and yet reaches out in longing across that void.

Yet there were limits to how much they would learn from their own theology of infinite love. Though they lived just across the border from Nazi Germany, von Speyr and von Balthasar seemed unable to see how their radical theology demanded a radical political response to the fascism just outside their door. This chapter reads their theology against their politics, finding in their description of the Trinity a profoundly antifascist politics that they themselves could not see—a theology we desperately need in our own moment. Insisting that love is constituted by otherness and relation across separation, their trinitarian theology of mourning grounds a better way of navigating difference than either liberal "welcome culture" or right-wing xenophobia, and pushes us toward more radical acts of solidarity in the twilight of the Christian West.

☙

Simone Weil described creation as an act of withdrawal in which God voids a space where the world can arise. Adrienne von Speyr takes us one step back. Before

God is estranged from the world, she writes, God is estranged from Godself. The absence separating God from creation is nested in a more fundamental absence separating God the Father from God the Son. (While in this chapter I follow von Speyr and von Balthasar in using the traditional gendered language of Father and Son, it is important to note this language, like all merely human language grasping at divine things, only gestures at what it can never hope to capture. We could just as rightly follow Julian of Norwich and call all three persons of the Trinity "Mother.")

Mixing her metaphors a bit, von Speyr writes that the relationship between God the Father and God the Son is like that between two spouses on the eve of one of them leaving on a voyage. Before saying goodbye for who knows how long, the two "consider their love and reaffirm it for the future beyond the coming separation." When two who love separate, "however bitter the time of loneliness may be, something remains that draws them together over and above all separation."[8] They are apart, but their longing binds them no matter how great the distance between them, and so their absence from each other is itself the paradoxical presence of their love. The estrangement itself is neces-

8. Adrienne von Speyr, *The Farewell Discourses: Meditations on John 13–17*, trans. E. A. Nelson (San Francisco: Ignatius Press, 1987), 337.

sary: for there to be love between them, there must be a *between*; there must be an absence.

Describing the love between God and God as like two lovers waving goodbye as one pulls away from shore, von Speyr marks absence and yearning and sorrow as at the heart of the Trinity. And her description of God's love as erotic yearning has a long precedent in Christian mystical theology. In von Balthasar's hands, this yearning will take on more explicitly the color of mourning. But for both, to say God is love is to say God is longing.

Christian mystics have long used erotic language to describe God's love. Drawing on the intense and sorrowful yearning that haunts the Song of Songs ("Upon my bed at night I sought him whom my soul loves; I sought him but found him not" [3:1]) and combining it with Greek philosophical and poetic reflection on love, Christian mystics have often named the love that is God *eros*. When the New Testament names God love, the word used in Greek is *agape*. Ask any seminarian, and they will tell you that ancient Greek had many words for love. There's *eros*, or longing; *agape*, or universal love; *philia*, or love between friends; *philautia*, or love of self; *storge*, or affection; and on and on. But anyone who has lived and loved can tell our seminarian that these aren't so easy to distinguish. Love exceeds classification. And so early in Christian history, theologians like Origen of Alexandria and Pseudo-Dionysius insisted that these words are synonyms. "You must take whatever Scripture says about [*agape*]," Origen wrote, "as if it had been said with reference to [*eros*], taking no note of the difference of terms; for the same meaning is conveyed by both."[9]

When the Scripture writers call God *agape*, they could just as easily have called God *eros*. And *eros*, as the classicist and poet Anne Carson points out, is about absence. "On the surface of it," Carson writes, "the lover wants the beloved." But "this, of course, is not really the case. . . . Union would be annihilating."[10] Think of any love in your own life. While of course on some level you desire to draw nearer to the one you love, it's the distance, that gap between *you* and *them* that makes you two different people, that makes love possible. Love is not a journey toward sameness, as if one day you and your beloved will look back and say, "We did it, we're not different anymore!" Were there no separation—the same thoughts, the same feelings, the same perspective—there would be no *them* for you to love. To "have" them in this way would be to truly, utterly lose them. Instead love requires accepting a persistent absence of

9. Origen, *An Exhortation to Martyrdom, Prayer, and Selected Works*, trans. Rowan A. Greer, The Classics of Western Spirituality (New York: Paulist Press, 1979), 227.

10. Anne Carson, *Eros the Bittersweet: An Essay* (Princeton, NJ: Princeton University Press, 1988), 62.

the other, accepting that while you will forever reach for them they will forever remain lost to your reach.

Von Speyr's image of two people waving goodbye as the distance between them grows illustrates that love is always consenting to be two however much the two might wish to be one, loving the void that holds them apart as what makes possible the love between them in the first place. It's not surprising then that Carson, describing the want and lack at the heart of every love, uses strikingly trinitarian language: "Conjoined they are held apart. The third component plays a paradoxical role for it both connects and separates, marking that two are not one, irradiating the absence whose presence is demanded by eros."[11] Void and lack and otherness are not obstacles that love promises to overcome, but the very stuff of love. Every love is already a grief, and no less love for that.

⌘

Love is want and lack, loss and absence. So where von Speyr reaches for images of romantic longing, von Balthasar turns to mourning. Translating her mystical theology into the academic language of systematic theology, he dwells at length on the theology of the Trinity—which for von Balthasar is always the theology of

11. Carson, *Eros the Bittersweet,* 16.

the cross. Von Balthasar describes God's infinitude not in terms of infinite power or infinite knowledge, but in terms of the infinite reach of God's love—a love capable of reaching even that which is infinitely removed from Godself, capable of reaching into the absolute zero point of utter godlessness.[12] And so, for von Balthasar, God's love is most fully realized on Holy Saturday. On that day the love between God and God is stretched to an infinite grief.

Since the first centuries of Christianity, popular narratives have sprung up about what exactly Jesus was up to between Good Friday and Easter Sunday. The most dramatic of these stories tell of the "harrowing of hell," in which Jesus knocks down the gates of hell, ties up the devil, and leads (some of) the underworld's captive souls free. But for von Balthasar, these stories miss the whole point of Holy Saturday. Describing a superhero Jesus fighting the devil, they cordon off some threshold of nothingness to which Jesus will not be reduced. The Jesus of the harrowing stories isn't *really* dead. He's more active than ever as he marches through the underworld, godlike and radiant next to the righteous few he unfetters and the moaning shades he leaves behind. There are depths to which this Jesus does not descend. For von

12. Hans Urs von Balthasar, *Mysterium Paschale: The Mystery of Easter*, trans. Aiden Nichols (Edinburgh: T&T Clark, 1990), 28.

Balthasar, conversely, the meaning of Holy Saturday is Jesus's "solidarity with the dead," his descent into the absolute godforsakenness of real death.[13]

Real death: Jesus between Good Friday and Easter Sunday is for von Balthasar a corpse like any other, moldering in the tomb, forsaken and abandoned to the corruption of nothingness. In the gloomy theological picture von Balthasar paints, the fact that Jesus sunk to such a depth of godlessness is the very bedrock of our faith. *Even this* is not beyond the reach of God's love. Love reaches *even here*, even to the nothingness of a corpse. "It is *he* who sets the limits to the extension of damnation, who forms the boundary stone marking the place where the lowest pitch is reached."[14] At the furthest possible remove from God, as the boundary stone marking infinite godforsakenness, lies—God.

The utter deadness of Jesus and the mourning love that unites dead Son and grieving Father means this: it is simply not possible to fall outside the span of God's love. This is a love that extends all the way from God to that which has been infinitely cast off from God.

Not that the horror is in any way lessened. But it is reached. There is no depth of abjection into which one person can plunge another, no distance from God to

13. Von Balthasar, *Mysterium Paschale,* 165.
14. Von Balthasar, *Mysterium Paschale,* 167.

which our sin can drag us, that would lie beyond this boundary stone. The infinite love of God is for von Balthasar and von Speyr a love that longs across a truly infinite separation. On the cross, von Speyr writes, Jesus "emptied himself until his whole self was nothing but a burning void."[15] God is for her an endless void, an everlasting and everreaching grief.

೦೨

Here von Speyr and von Balthasar give us a trinitarian structure for a theology of mourning, and give hints as to the political demands of such a theology. The "divine act that brings forth the Son," writes von Balthasar, "involves the positing of an absolute, infinite 'distance' that can contain and embrace all other distances that are possible within the world of finitude."[16] Within God's infinite distance from God are all the distances and differences within creation.

The Father sends the Son away—and the Father doesn't exist prior to this sending; instead, the Father *just is* this act of absolute renunciation. "He will not be God for himself alone," von Balthasar writes. As the

15. Adrienne von Speyr, *The Cross: Word and Sacrament*, 2nd ed. (San Francisco: Ignatius Press, 2017), 53.

16. Hans Urs von Balthasar, *Theo-Drama: Theological Dramatic Theory, Volume IV: The Action*, trans. Graham Harrison (San Francisco: Ignatius Press, 1988), 323–24.

Father turns away from himself and toward the Son he has sent, the Son turns away from himself and toward the Father who sent him in "a thanksgiving as selfless and unreserved as the Father's original self-surrender."[17] As in Carson's description of eros, Father and Son consent to be two and not one. For there to be love between them, they must be separate. And for there to be *infinite* love between God and God, this separation must likewise be infinite.

And yet because God *is* love, this absolute separation is itself paradoxically the closest intimacy. Using the language of academic theology, von Balthasar distinguishes between the "immanent Trinity," or who God is in relation to Godself, and the "economic Trinity," or who God is in relation to the world. The infinite separation of Father from Son is how God's love appears in the economic Trinity. The Son is sent to the furthest possible distance from the Father, and the Holy Spirit "appears in the form of mere distance," as von Balthasar puts it. The Spirit appears as loss itself. But in the immanent Trinity, this loss appears as intimacy, in that the distance between them is bridged by the love they share.[18]

The Holy Spirit is for von Balthasar like what Carson calls "the absent presence of desire," the third that

17. Von Balthasar, *Theo-Drama*, 4:323–24.
18. Von Balthasar, *Theo-Drama*, 4:320.

at once connects and separates Father and Son.[19] "Proceeding from both, as their subsistent 'We,'" von Balthasar writes, "there breathes the 'Spirit' who is common to both: as the essence of love, he maintains the infinite difference between them, seals it and, since he is the one Spirit of them both, bridges it."[20]

It's here, with this idea of an infinite difference within God that contains all finite differences in creation, that we begin to glimpse the political challenge of von Speyr and von Balthasar's theology of the Trinity. Contained within God's longing are all the finite distances and differences between creatures. This world, proliferating with difference as well as suffering, is itself the absent presence of God's desire. Every gap holding us apart and different from others is thus the presence in the world of finitude of God's infinite longing, God's mourning for God. To demand others become less different, or to insist distance forecloses the possibility of relation, is to refuse to be drawn into this longing love. A politics informed by von Speyr and von Balthasar's theology of the Trinity would cherish the differences and distances between us as finite glimpses of the infinite void of God's love.

༝

19. Carson, *Eros the Bittersweet*, 30.
20. Von Balthasar, *Theo-Drama*, 4:323–24.

As I mentioned, neither von Speyr nor von Balthasar themselves held to such a politics. Though they lived at the same time as the other antifascist writers discussed in this book, they stayed frustratingly aloof from the political crises roiling around them.

I find their silence impossible to understand, let alone excuse. They even spent the 1930s and '40s in Basel, the same city just on the border with Nazi Germany where Karl Barth was leveling his theological critique of fascism. Yet they kept quiet. And while von Balthasar wrote an essay against antisemitism in the late hour of 1943, that essay hardly makes up for another he wrote in 1940 praising the Nazi regime's policies against "degenerate art."[21] Where von Balthasar waffled, von Speyr kept silent. Still, their theology remains in excess of their political failures. Though they could not or would not see it, their theology of the Trinity has radical antifascist implications.

Judith Butler, in their essay on Hannah Arendt's *Eichmann in Jerusalem*, writes that the Nazis' fundamental crime was that they "took as their own right the decision with whom to share the earth."[22] An antifascist

21. Peter Joseph Fritz, "Balthasar, the Sublime, and the Avant-Garde," *Modern Theology*, March 13, 2022, https://doi.org/10.1111/moth.12784.

22. Judith Butler, "Hannah Arendt's Death Sentences," *Comparative Literature Studies* 48, no. 3 (2011): 280–95, 287.

ethic, for Butler, is one in which we consent to share the world with those we did not choose, those we would not have chosen had anyone asked us, which of course nobody did. As the climate crisis continues to shrink the habitable earth and the decision not to share only becomes more tempting, we need to learn now how to consent to share the earth with those we did not choose. Von Speyr and von Balthasar's trinitarian theology pushes us toward just such a radical antifascist ethic, despite their own failure to meet the demands of their own moment. So let's take von Speyr and von Balthasar's theology where they would not go themselves.

ॐ

Von Speyr and von Balthasar's trinitarian theology insists that estrangement and difference are not obstacles that love strives to overcome but are instead the absent presence of love itself. This idea finds a curious echo in the moral and political thought of the Caribbean poet and philosopher Édouard Glissant. Glissant ends his 1990 book *Poetics of Relation* with a call: "We clamor for the right to opacity for everyone."[23] Often, he laments, those positioned as the West's others—non-

23. Édouard Glissant, *Poetics of Relation*, trans. Betsy Wing (Ann Arbor: University of Michigan Press, 1997), 194. My reading of Glissant is indebted to Benjamin P. Davis, *Choose Your*

Christians, people of color, queer people, immigrants—
are compelled to be "transparent," to make themselves
knowable, meaning make themselves less other. Those
beyond the walls of the Christian West are seen as too
strange, too unfamiliar, too opaque, with their inscru-
table languages and their foreign gods and their dark
skin. They must be made transparent so that they can
be better "known" by the Western subject. And as
Theodor Adorno wrote, "Understood in its full implications, to 'know' men is to despise them: 'That's the
way they are, and that's that.'"[24] Transparency becomes
either the condition for inclusion ("I know you, you're
not so different after all") or the excuse for rejection ("I
know you, you don't belong here").

Today, liberal welcome culture and right-wing xenophobia are two sides of this demand for transparency:
either strangers are welcome here so long as they act
like good Westerners and make themselves useful, or
they're welcome to remain different so long as they stay
on the other side of the border (and keep the commodi-
ties coming). Either be here and don't be different, or be
different and don't be here.

Bearing: Édouard Glissant, Human Rights and Decolonial Ethics
(Edinburgh: Edinburgh University Press, 2023).

24. Theodor W. Adorno, *Prisms* (Cambridge, MA: MIT Press,
1982), 61, https://doi.org/10.7551/mitpress/5570.001.0001.

This demand for transparency doesn't only have to do with borders. The greater inclusion extended to gay and trans people over the last decades has come with a demand to be less different: get married, raise children, join the military. Those who remain opaque remain excluded and abandoned. Across the political spectrum, approaches to difference too often refuse what Glissant calls opacity: the confounding, unknowable, unassimilable *otherness* of another person, that which can never be understood, that which keeps someone always "them" and never "me."

Respecting the right to opacity is, for Glissant, the great dilemma of moral and political life. It's a dilemma because we're always caught on two horns: how to relate to another person without that relation flattening out their difference, and how to preserve another's difference without that consent to separateness becoming an excuse for refusing relation. Liberal welcome culture is caught on the first horn, while the right-wing project of global segregation is caught on the second. The right to opacity for Glissant names the riddle at the heart of politics today: how to hold together relation and difference, intimacy and estrangement.

Édouard Glissant would have as little interest in debates on how the immanent Trinity relates to the economic Trinity as Adrienne von Speyr and Hans Urs von Balthasar would have in the avant-garde decolonial poetics of *creolité*. But read them together, and a theological response to the dilemma of difference starts to become visible.

The dilemma starts to look less like a beast with two horns if we ground relation in the three-part love of the Trinity. The love between God and God, for our Swiss theologians, is always at once greatest intimacy and greatest estrangement, greatest intimacy *because* greatest estrangement, because loss and difference and distance are constitutive of love itself. The trinitarian love of God is not threatened by otherness and loss but is made real in mournful desire.

Lived out in the world, this kind of love would look like what Jacques Derrida calls "unconditional hospitality." Unconditional hospitality, he acknowledges, carries real risks, "terrible" and perhaps "unbearable" risks.[25] To truly welcome another person without conditions is to open oneself to the possibility of being taken advantage of, of being harmed. In the coming years of the Greatest Migration, we will hear more and more about these risks. But genuine, unconditional hospitality requires opening ourselves to risk. Von Speyr and von Balthasar's trinitarian theology makes clear that the love that is God is not a self-enclosed love for the

25. Derrida, "Hospitality, Justice and Responsibility," 70.

same, but love across a real distance, love for what is really different.

Living out that longing love requires opening ourselves to the risks inherent in relation with someone who is genuinely other. "Those are the risks involved in pure hospitality," Derrida wrote, "if there is such a thing, and I am not sure that there is."[26] I'm not sure either. But if we are to live a life shaped after God's love and to share that love with others, then such unconditional hospitality is demanded of us. Maybe this time we actually can do this.

26. Derrida, "Hospitality, Justice and Responsibility," 70.

PART 2

Corpus Mysticum

Lyon, 1944

In a crumbling shed on the estate of an old boarding school slept a priest in his late forties. It had been four years since the Nazis invaded France. Two years since Lyon fell. For two long years, the city had been under the thumb of the sadistic Gestapo leader Klaus Barbie, "the Butcher of Lyon." From his headquarters in the Hôtel Terminus, Barbie transformed the city into a vast archipelago of torture chambers, its streets teeming with informants and spies. Resisters, suspected resisters, Jews, suspected Jews, even children—Barbie's torturers swept up anyone and everyone.

The priest lifted himself off his cot and coughed. His joints were stiff after another sleepless night. He dragged his bleary eyes across the ramshackle shed one last time before rolling up his blanket and stepping out onto the frozen grass. He left the door open. Let the animals come in, let them cover the tracks.

Father Henri de Lubac was on the run. He had been involved in antifascist work before the invasion, but

81

when Barbie seized the city the resistance scattered and went underground. Contact was kept to a minimum to ensure those captured and tortured would give up as few comrades as possible. Still, de Lubac and a handful of friends started a clandestine journal, the Cahiers du Témoignage chrétien. *From its pages they would level an idiosyncratic critique of fascism as a kind of heresy, not the return to paganism it often claimed to be but a twisted form of Christianity.*

Their work made them targets. Communicating in code, meeting in secret locations, always wary of traps and betrayals, furtively passing documents in the dead of night. Eventually they were discovered.

A man and woman showed up at de Lubac's door, harried and dressed in rags, begging for safe passage out of France. Could he show them an escape route? But things were so uncertain, and that route might be cut off—could he show them others? All of the escape routes, actually, just to be safe? And could he give the names of others in the resistance, in case something went wrong?

It was time to leave. A friend let him stay in the old shed for a while, but they would find it soon enough. So he skipped town. One by one his friends were captured, tortured, deported, killed.

Yet amid all this, eking out a meager survival on the run, de Lubac would surface from time to time, meeting with publishers and desperately trying to publish a manuscript he had been working on for years. The risks were incalculable. French publishers were all too compliant with the regime's censors. Any of these meetings could have been a trap. But for de Lubac, the risks were worth it. The book needed to get out. Eventually, in 1944, under the unblinking gaze of the censors, his book was published: Corpus Mysticum: The Church and the Eucharist in the Middle Ages.

❧

At first glance, it's not clear why someone would risk everything (why someone would risk anything) to publish a book like *Corpus Mysticum*. It's not even much of a book, more a jumble of citations and footnotes, sources piled on sources, barely held together from section to section.

The purpose of the book was to exhaustively document a subtle shift in eucharistic language from the ninth to the thirteenth century. All of eucharistic theology, de Lubac wrote, is a meditation on the mysterious "unity of the 'three bodies' of Christ."[1] We use the phrase "the Body of Christ" to refer at once to the individual body of Jesus of Nazareth, the consecrated bread

1. Henri de Lubac, *Corpus Mysticum: The Eucharist and the Church in the Middle Ages*, trans. Gemma Simmonds (Notre Dame, IN: University of Notre Dame Press, 2007), 260.

of the Eucharist, and the church community; when
that community gathers to break that bread in memory
of that man's death, we enter into the mystery that all
three of these are in fact one. De Lubac's book began
with the observation that, before the ninth century, the
phrase "the mystical body," or *corpus mysticum*, was
used to refer to the consecrated bread. The book then
went on to describe how, after the thirteenth century,
that phrase came to refer to the church, with the bread
now called Christ's "true body" or *corpus verum*.

That's it.

For this, de Lubac was willing to risk everything. He
was willing to risk torture and death, was willing to risk
betraying his comrades, all to document this obscure
moment in the history of medieval eucharistic theology. *Corpus Mysticum* was as important to him as his
resistance activity. More than that: for him, the book
was resistance activity.

In an underground essay in 1942, de Lubac wrote that
"the idea of the [Third] Reich is itself conceived after
the fashion of the idea of the mystical Body in Christianity."[2] To understand and undermine the Reich, you
had to understand and undermine the theology prop-
ping it up. Developments in medieval eucharistic theol-

2. Henri de Lubac, *Résistance chrétienne au nazisme*, ed.
Renée Bédarida and Jacques Prévotat, in *Œuvres complètes
XXXIV* (Paris: Editions du Cerf, 2006), 289.

ogy might not only help explain the fascist conception of the body politic; dissenting voices from that same period might offer strategies for resistance.

De Lubac wasn't alone in this line of reasoning. Around the same time, Simone Weil was working out similar ideas. It's not clear if she ever read any of de Lubac's work, but in May 1942 she was in Marseilles distributing an issue of *Témoignage chrétien*'s journal edited by de Lubac himself. And that same month, she wrote in a letter to a friend that fascist politics hinged on a "judicious transposition" from theology to politics of thirteenth-century ideas of the *corpus mysticum*.[3] The two antifascist theologians were circling around a similar idea. Convoluted as it may seem, for Weil, de Lubac, and others in the orbit of *Témoignage chrétien*, there was something about the theology of the *corpus mysticum* as it developed in the thirteenth century that structured all of modern Western politics and made possible the racial-nationalist political imaginary of twentieth-century fascism. An article in that same May 1942 journal laid out the stakes. The article quoted a Vichy official who justified France's new anti-Jewish laws by claiming that the regime was merely carrying forward laws from the Middle Ages. The article's anonymous author admitted that the government official

3. Weil, *Waiting for God*, 41.

had a point: the fascist powers were in fact reviving ideas and practices from medieval Christianity. And yet, the author insisted, precisely because of the medieval theological heritage of modern politics, the diversity of medieval theology contained possible resources for political resistance. The struggle against fascism, the article claimed, recapitulated a medieval struggle between a twisted "gospel of hate" and the true "gospel of love."[4]

The shift in eucharistic theology that de Lubac's book traces, when from the ninth to the thirteenth century "the mystical body" went from referring to the consecrated bread to the church community, had in his eyes political effects that culminated in twentieth-century fascism.[5] By the thirteenth century, Christian community came to be imagined as the mystical "expression" of Christ's "true body," which was made present in the bread during the eucharistic rite. It's not just that the church was imagined as a communal body: now that body had a visible pattern to shape itself after. And the

4. *Cahiers clandestins du Témoignage chrétien* (Paris: Éditions du Témoignage Chrétien, 1946), 215–16.
5. The story of how this shift informed the political imaginary of the modern European nation-state is told in Ernst H. Kantorowicz, *The King's Two Bodies: A Study in Medieval Political Theology* (Princeton, NJ: Princeton University Press, 2016), 193–272.

eucharistic bread, as the "true body" of Christ, was in the thirteenth century the focus of increasing anxiety around its purity and homogeneity.

Innumerable pamphlets were written about what variety of wheat could make up the bread, what specific equipment could be used, which recipes were approved and which forbidden, who is allowed to carry the bread and wine, what should be done if crumbs fell or drops were spilled.[6] It was this kind of body that Christian society was imagined to "mystically" express: a fragile site of purity and holiness in a corrupt and hostile world, a body with rigid and visible boundaries that made it possible, when the priest lifted it above the altar, to easily see where it ended and the rest of the world began.

Thus, at the same time, in the thirteenth century, Christian society in Western Europe subjected itself to an increasingly violent regime of communal purification to make itself better conform to the ideal of the visible and bounded *corpus verum*.[7] This effort received its official proclamation in the Fourth Lateran Council

6. Caroline Walker Bynum, *Holy Feast and Holy Fast: The Religious Significance of Food to Medieval Women* (Los Angeles: University of California Press, 1987); Miri Rubin, *Corpus Christi: The Eucharist in Late Medieval Culture* (New York: Cambridge University Press, 1991).

7. Frederick Christian Bauerschmidt, *Julian of Norwich and the Mystical Body Politic of Christ* (Notre Dame, IN: University of Notre Dame Press, 1999), https://muse.jhu.edu/book/7338.

of 1215. The council lamented that Jews and Muslims were difficult to visually distinguish from Christians. One could not see the boundaries of the *corpus mysticum* as easily as one could see the boundaries of the *corpus verum*. So it was decreed that non-Christians would be forced to wear special clothing identifying them as outsiders.[8] The social body of Christendom would be made to resemble the "true body" that it was said to "mystically" express: pure, homogeneous, with rigid and visible borders.

This connection between the church as mystical body and the bread as real body had deadly consequences. Fears that Jews were infiltrating the *corpus mysticum* were mirrored in rumors they were stealing and desecrating the sacramental bread—the former led to the yellow star, the latter led to massacres.

For de Lubac and his comrades, the racist nationalism of their own day was heir to this medieval eucharistic anxiety: the social body of the Third Reich was imagined to mystically express the idealized Aryan body, and those who could not or would not conform to that body were expelled or eliminated. The Nazis' revival of the yellow star and the pogrom were undeniable proof for de Lubac that the political crisis gripping

8. Henry Joseph Schroeder, *Disciplinary Decrees of the General Councils: Text, Translation and Commentary* (St. Louis: B. Herder, 1937), 236–96.

Europe had deep roots in this little-remembered episode of theological history.

Yet as the anonymous author of that *Témoignage chrétien* article pointed out, theology in the medieval period was not monolithic. Alongside the reigning "gospel of hate," other voices murmured a different "gospel of love." And this other theological tradition had its own eucharistic theologies. If de Lubac was right that modern Western politics, including the politics of fascism, are stuck within the dynamic of *corpus verum* and *corpus mysticum* as it developed by the thirteenth century, then eucharistic theologies from that century might ground a politics of resistance. Other theologies of *corpus verum* and *corpus mysticum* proliferated in the thirteenth century, lying in wait to be taken up anew and wielded against the fascist body politic.

༚

Inspired by de Lubac's antifascist medievalism, this section looks to how medieval eucharistic theology might both aid our understanding of today's political crises and inspire resistance. In the chapters that follow, we'll look at the eucharistic theologies of two thirteenth-century women: Hadewijch, a woman from the region of present-day Belgium, and Angela of Foligno, from central Italy. Bringing their theologies of the mystical body to bear on today's racist and nationalist articulations of the body politic will further our understanding of how a theology of mourning can help us navigate the twilight of the Christian West.

The work of mourning demands both reckoning irrevocable loss and moving forward into a future in which new loves are possible, as in the angel's words at the empty tomb: "He is not here; he has gone to Galilee." Hadewijch dwells in that first aspect, "He is not here," the mourner's unsatisfied longing for a lost love. For her, the love that is God is a desire that remains forever unsatisfied. The Eucharist offers the "real presence" of Christ not because it satisfies our desire for him, but because it *doesn't* satisfy that desire, because it deepens our longing for one who is absent and thus makes viscerally present to us the unsatisfied longing that God only ever is. Hadewijch's eucharistic theology can help us reframe our relationship to the loss of that other of Christ's "three bodies," the church. With Hadewijch as our guide we can see the sorrowful longing stirred by the loss of that body as itself participation in the longing love of God.

Angela moves us into the second aspect of mourning, "He has gone to Galilee," the opening out toward new loves. She also deepens for us the political challenge of the theology of mourning. If every social body is to some extent founded through exclusion—if every "us" requires a "them"—Angela insists that our always unsatisfied desire for Christ should drive us beyond any line drawn around a so-called Christian form of life out toward what has been excluded.

For de Lubac, Weil, and the other courageous resisters around the *Témoignage chrétien* group, thirteenth-century eucharistic theology was a vital resource for understanding and resisting racist and nationalist conceptions of the body politic. Hadewijch and Angela have not been as influential for Christian theology as their contemporaries Thomas Aquinas, Duns Scotus, or Bonaventure. But their writings are like roads not traveled for theology, offering alternate ways of thinking about Christian community that we can return to in the twilight of the Christian West, when calls to defend pure, visible, and rigidly bordered forms of Christian community are growing ever-more violent. Read together, these two women offer a politically radical theology of mourning in which the end of the Christian West can be seen as a way of participating in the self-effacing love of God.

CHAPTER 3

Hadewijch
Losing the Body of Christ

In the spring of 2020 I was living in Chelsea, Massachusetts, a working-class, immigrant city just north of Boston. COVID hit the city harder than almost anywhere else in the country. Much of Chelsea lives below the poverty line, working in food processing and packaging industries that classed them as "essential workers" and forced them to work long hours for low pay in crowded and poorly ventilated areas. Many Chelseans are also undocumented, or live with undocumented relatives, which made them understandably wary of interacting with state health workers during the first Trump administration. These conditions let the virus rip through Chelsea. So the priest at my parish decided early on to move our church services online. To preserve our neighbors from harm as best we could, we would begin a long eucharistic fast.

During that time, as the death toll of my neighbors mounted, the sense of precarity and loss deepened, and

the grief and isolation of that long sacramental deprivation dragged on, I read again and again the work of
the medieval theologian Hadewijch. Her work explores
the paradoxical mixture of joy and anguish, communion and loneliness, contained in the central Christian
claim *God is love*. The word for "love" in her Middle
Dutch dialect, the feminine noun *Minne*, is bewilder-
ingly complex, naming at once feeling and action, lover
and beloved, the space that holds us apart and the love
that reaches out across that space.[1]

Most important for Hadewijch is that reaching, the
desire that is the beating heart of any love. The riddle
her theology endlessly turns over is that love reaches
for union, for the satisfaction of desire that would make
two into one; yet satisfaction is the end of desire—and a
love without desire would be no love at all. Thus while
love seems to strive for union, it in fact lives in distance
and difference. To say God is infinite love, to name God
Minne, is to say that God's love for us and our love for
God is an infinite longing that remains forever unsatisfied.

Hadewijch's writings weave this idea of God's love as
longing with classic mystical tropes of union with God
into a paradoxical theology in which we can "have" God

1. Emily A. Holmes, *Flesh Made Word: Medieval Women
Mystics, Writing, and the Incarnation* (Waco, TX: Baylor University Press, 2013), 47.

only when we lack God and go on yearning in the void. She explores this paradox primarily through eucharistic language, depicting the sacrament as "feeding" her with the real presence of God precisely by withholding this presence, by *not* satisfying her hunger for God—because the God who is *Minne* is present only as desire itself, as want and lack, as a hunger that goes unfed.

This tangled logic in which God is present only in and as God's absence is why I found her writings so vital during those pandemic months of sacramental deprivation. Unable to take the Eucharist, bereft of my church community, and despairing at the endless litany of losses, I felt starved of God. But for Hadewijch, unsatisfied hunger for God is what the sacrament is all about in the first place.

Through Hadewijch's eucharistic theology of *Minne*, I saw mourning the loss of the body of Christ as itself a way of being pulled deeper into the longing love of God. For those of us living in the twilight of the Christian West, Hadewijch can help us mourn the loss of that other body of Christ: the ecclesial body, those familiar forms of Christian community that have been so central to Western societies and that are now dying out. Rather than demanding that our desire for the body of Christ be satisfied by imposing a "Christian culture" through force, we might with Hadewijch see the loss of any such possibility of satisfaction—our mourning for

Christ's absent body—as itself the strange presence of God's longing love.

༚

Last names are a recent invention, so premodern people are usually known by the place they lived: Julian of Norwich, Origen of Alexandria, Thomas Aquinas. But Hadewijch is just Hadewijch. We know almost nothing about her life. Given her dialect of Middle Dutch, she must have lived somewhere near present-day Belgium. And given her influence on the fourteenth-century theologian John of Ruysbroeck, she must have lived sometime in the thirteenth century. That's pretty much it. (We don't even know how to pronounce her name. I've heard three Hadewijch scholars say it three different ways. I say "Hod-vick," which is probably wrong.) Despite how little we know about her, many of her writings have survived—letters, mystical visions, poems, songs.

It was costly and time-consuming to copy manuscripts in the Middle Ages, and even more so to translate them, so we know she was regarded as an intellectual authority in her own day. But though her ideas continued to subtly influence theology, by the middle of the sixteenth century her name and writings were almost entirely forgotten. Then, in 1838, three medievalists working in the Royal Library in Brussels stumbled on a fourteenth-century manuscript where scrawled in the margins by some unknown copyist was a name: "Beata Hadewigis." Blessed Hadewijch.[2]

The writings collected in that manuscript form a theology that plumbs the bottomless depth of the claim that God is love. "I constantly wished to know," Hadewijch writes in the second of her fourteen visions, "and kept thinking of it, and repeated ceaselessly: 'What is love? And who is love?'"[3] Love, *Minne* in her Middle Dutch, is not a simple thing. On the one hand, love involves the coming together of lover and beloved, two becoming one. As she writes in a letter, in love "neither of the two distinguishes himself from the other. But they abide in one another in fruition, mouth in mouth, heart in heart, body in body, and soul in soul." Yet this coming together, this "fruition," is always frustrated. Recall Adrienne von Speyr and Hans Urs von Balthasar's theology of the Trinity. Like them, Hadewijch knows that if there is to be love between lover and beloved, there must be a space between. Lover and beloved must remain somehow distinct; their longing to become one must never be satisfied.

2. Hadewijch, "Introduction," in *The Complete Works*, trans. Columba Hart (New York: Paulist Press, 1980), 2.

3. Hadewijch, "Vision 2," in *The Complete Works*, 271.

The nuances of Hadewijch's Middle Dutch let her explore this paradox of coming together and remaining apart, as she insists on the identity of fruition, or *ghebruken*, and separation, or *ghebreken*.[4] Lover and beloved "are both one thing through each other, but at the same time remain two different selves—yes, and remain so forever."[5] Recall Anne Carson's insight that though in love two desire to become one, "union would be annihilating."[6] The only way to keep love alive is to accept that the beloved will always exceed your grasp, that to love is always at the same time to lose. Hadewijch's genius lies in drawing out the theological import of this inseparability of love and loss. Writing in the thirteenth century, the same time period in which (as Henri de Lubac described) Christian society in Western Europe was imagining itself as the mystical expression of a "true body" in which all goodness and purity were visibly present, Hadewijch instead turns toward lack, longing, and absence. If God is love, and if love requires separation, then our relationship to God and God's relationship to us must look more like not-having

---

4. Holly Hillgardner, *Longing and Letting Go: Christian and Hindu Practices of Passionate Non-Attachment*, American Academy of Religion Academy Series (New York: Oxford University Press, 2017), 52–70.

5. Hadewijch, "Letter 9," in *The Complete Works*, 66.

6. Carson, *Eros the Bittersweet*, 62.

than having, more like longing than union, more like mourning than possession.

ॐ

In the twilight of the Christian West, when our relationship to the body of Christ is more grief and loss than communion and presence, Hadewijch's writings reveal how our mourning might teach us something new. She explores the paradoxical identity of presence and absence, love and loss, *ghebruken* and *ghebreken*, that make up any love relationship. And in naming God *Minne*, she reads this overlapping of love and loss into the very fabric of the world. "Nothing can dwell in [*Minne*]," she writes in a letter to a friend, "and nothing can touch her except desire."[7] (Given *Minne* is a feminine noun, Hadewijch frequently uses female pronouns for God.) If the love that is God is this kind of forever-unsatisfied desire, then we draw near to God not when our desire for God is satisfied but when it is frustrated and deepened. God's love is longing, and we long for what we lack, so we are pulled into the love of God precisely when we lack God and go on longing.

Hadewijch is well aware of how this paradox is at once exhilarating and painful. Her poetry vividly captures the ecstasy and anguish of desire, all the while insist-

7. Hadewijch, "Letter 20," in *The Complete Works*, 91.

ing that in mourning God's absence she approaches the strange presence of a God who is longing. "Her concealment reveals what can be known of her," she writes of God. "Her withdrawal is approach. . . . Her wealth is her lack of everything. . . . Her table is hunger; her knowledge is error. . . . Her revelation is the total hiding of herself." God's table is hunger because the object of our desire is itself an infinite desire. Hadewijch returns again and again to this paradoxical image in which eating God only deepens our hunger, writing that "to die of hunger for [*Minne*] is to feed and taste."[8]

Theologians often write about God's superabundant being, but in Hadewijch's theology what is abundant is instead the lack that stirs an ever-greater craving. Hadewijch's visions describe a paradoxical union with a paradoxical God, where "hunger" is itself "feeding and tasting," where mourning God's absence delivers us the longing love that God only ever is.

This is why I read Hadewijch so avidly during that season of sacramental deprivation. With her images of eating and hunger, her theology of *Minne* offers a sophisticated eucharistic theology in which mourning and loss are themselves constitutive of the love that is God. One of her most vivid mystical visions occurred

8. Hadewijch, "Poem in Couplets 13," in *The Complete Works*, 344–45.

during morning prayers, when she saw Christ appear and administer the sacrament to her. She writes that she experienced union with Christ in this moment, "as if we were one without difference."[9] Yet at the very moment when it seemed her desire was satisfied, her beloved disappeared. She then heard God's voice:

> Come, and be yourself the highest way. . . . Your great privation of Love has given you the highest way in the fruition of me. I have longed for this from the beginning of the world, and you have often paid for it with painful desire, and you will yet pay for it. This privation of what you desire above all, and this reaching out to me who am unreachable: This is the short hour that outvies all long hours. This is also the way that leads to my Nature, by which I came to myself and went forth.[10]

Receiving the sacrament, Hadewijch is given God's real presence, yet this is the presence of one whose nature is privation and painful desire. God is love, and love involves not-having, a difference and a distance between lover and beloved. So Hadewijch's experience

---

9. Hadewijch, "Vision 7," in *The Complete Works*, 281.
10. Hadewijch, "Vision 8," in *The Complete Works*, 283.

of mystical union with God in the Eucharist is union with that not-having itself, with that very difference and distance.

During those long months in 2020 when preserving our neighbors from harm meant going without the Eucharist, Hadewijch's theology of *Minne* helped me see my grief at lacking the body of Christ as a mysterious way into God's withdrawing love. And in the years to come, as the twilight of the Christian West continues to dim and the voices calling for its preservation through force grow louder, Hadewijch continues to hold open the possibility of a different way of relating to the loss of familiar Christian forms of community. Not a revolt against mourning, but a vision of Christian faith as itself a work of mourning—the *corpus mysticum* as a community of grieving love.

∾

Those pandemic months gave a glimpse of what sociologists in Western Europe and North America have been forecasting for a while now: a world after Western Christianity. The Episcopal Church, to which I belong, is dying faster than most. Political scientist Ryan P. Burge, analyzing the decline, noted that the church is on track to lose twenty-five thousand members each year to death while only baptizing ten thousand infants—

with only half of those infants expected to remain in the church through adulthood.[11] Things are less dire for other denominations, but only by degree. In Europe as in the United States, Christianity is dwindling away.[12]

Hadewijch's sophisticated eucharistic theology offers a way to mourn this loss of the body of Christ. But some Christian thinkers are instead opting for a furious revolt against mourning, arguing that Christians in the West must tighten our grip on state power and wield it to shore up the faith against the corrosive acid of liberal individualism. This is the point of view often called the "postliberal right," articulated by bestselling authors like Sohrab Ahmari and Rod Dreher, academics like Notre Dame's Patrick Deneen and Harvard's Adrian Vermeule, theologians like Chad Pecknold, and think tankers like Gladden Pappin.

---

11. Ryan P. Burge, "The Death of the Episcopal Church Is Near," *Religion in Public* (blog), July 6, 2021, https://religionin public.blog/2021/07/06/the-death-of-the-episcopal-church-is-near/.

12. "Being Christian in Western Europe," *Pew Research Center* (blog), May 29, 2018, https://www.pewresearch.org/religion/2018/05/29/being-christian-in-western-europe/; "In U.S., Decline of Christianity Continues at Rapid Pace," *Pew Research Center* (blog), October 17, 2019, https://www.pewresearch.org/religion/2019/10/17/in-u-s-decline-of-christianity-continues-at-rapid-pace/.

This once-obscure movement has ascended to new heights of political power thanks to the election of J. D. Vance as vice president. Vance has described himself as a postliberal; he has spoken at postliberal conferences attended by Vermeule, Deneen, and Ahmari; and Dreher attended his baptism in 2019. This movement is gaining power, and its longing for a Christendom regained is worth taking seriously.

One thing that stands out when reading the postliberals' writings is how the end of the Christian West figures as an apocalyptic threat in the face of which almost anything becomes justifiable. In his 2017 book *The Benedict Option*, Rod Dreher warns that "there are people alive today who may live to see the effective death of Christianity within our civilization." He describes this anticipated loss in highly militarized language, as though anyone not a conservative Christian is an enemy combatant. The meager legal protections won by trans people over the last decade are "a harsh, relentless occupation" of Christian territory by anti-Christian forces. And those Christians who get too cozy with people different from themselves are traitors "aiding and abetting their own extinction."[13] Even an ostensibly serious academic like Patrick Deneen

13. Rod Dreher, *The Benedict Option: A Strategy for Christians in a Post-Christian Nation* (New York: Sentinel, 2017), 8, 3, 100.

veers into paranoid fantasies of imminent extermination when writing about the twilight of the Christian West. In his 2023 book *Regime Change*, Deneen claims that "classical liberal, progressive liberal, and Marxist ideologies [are] increasingly combining as a single power elite"—alleging a paranoid and incoherent conspiracy of Marxists and capitalists working together to keep "the people" down."[14] In a passage on "Critical Race Theory," Deneen accuses this shadowy elite of pursuing the "replacement" and even "effective elimination" of "white, heterosexual Christian men (and anyone sympathizing with them)."[15]

More staid is the Harvard law professor and leading light of the "integralist" wing of postliberal thought, Adrian Vermeule. Vermeule's more sophisticated critique of liberalism is that its insistence on maximal individual freedom is ultimately antisocial. Citizens of liberal regimes, he writes, are encouraged to see themselves not as members of a larger community (the family, the church, the nation) but as isolated individuals freely pursuing their isolated individual appetites in competition with one another. A "liberal community" is in Vermeule's view an oxymoron, and the impossibility of liberal community explains the various crises roiling

14. Patrick J. Deneen, *Regime Change: Toward a Postliberal Future* (New York: Sentinel, 2023), 130.
15. Deneen, *Regime Change*, 169.

the West today: atomization, loneliness, declining birth rates, and the desperate groping at ersatz community that is political tribalism.[16] Against this death drive of liberalism, Vermeule proposes what he calls "integration from within": Christians should seize the levers of state power within liberal societies and turn them against liberalism itself, "transform[ing] the decaying regime from within its own core" into a "postliberal" regime directed toward what Vermeule, in vague reference to Catholic social teaching, hazily refers to as "the common good."[17]

Vermeule offers hints as to what the common good means to him. In 2018, he and his fellow postliberal Chad Pecknold enthusiastically defended the nineteenth-century kidnapping by the Papal States of a six-year-old Jewish child named Edgardo Mortara, who had been baptized without his family's knowledge.[18] In

16. Adrian Vermeule, "The Ark of Tradition," *The Russell Kirk Center* (blog), November 19, 2017, https://kirkcenter.org/reviews/the-ark-of-tradition/.

17. Adrian Vermeule, "Integration from Within," *American Affairs Journal* (blog), February 20, 2018, https://americanaffairsjournal.org/2018/02/integration-from-within/.

18. Nathan Shields, "The Church's Once-Notorious Seizure of a Jewish Child Is Back. Why?," *Mosaic Magazine,* March 5, 2018, https://mosaicmagazine.com/essay/history-ideas/2018/03/the-churchs-once-notorious-seizure-of-a-jewish-child-is-back-why/.

Vermeule's hands, the concept of the common good is reduced to a cheap rhetorical trick to justify sovereign decisions on the body politic of a fantasized Christian civilization.

For postliberals like Deneen, Vermeule, Vance, and others, the twilight of the Christian West is a traumatic loss of the body of Christ that must be forestalled at seemingly any cost. However paranoid their descriptions of a "relentless occupation" of Christendom by trans people or their warnings about the coming "elimination" of straight, white Christian men might be, they are responding to something real: Christianity in the West really is on the decline, and we really do appear to be moving swiftly into a world after the Christian West. Yet as Freud wrote a century ago, "the proneness to decay of all that is beautiful" is leading the postliberals to "[cling] with all the greater intensity to what is left."[19]

The barest glimpse of a future in which church and sacrament will be absent from the world provokes in the postliberals a violent revolt against mourning, driving them to clutch at the levers of the state in order to crush into submission all those they see as undermining Christian culture: queer people, feminists, Muslims, immigrants, and (as seen in the defenses of the Mortara

19. Freud, "On Transience," 305, 307.

affair) Jews. Hadewijch's eucharistic theology scrambles the anxiety, most fevered among the postliberals but also haunting mainline and progressive Christians, that the church as body of Christ must be present and visible and protected from diminishment and loss.

Recall de Lubac's claim that eucharistic theology is always about the mysterious unity of Christ's "three bodies": the individual body of Jesus, the sacramental body of the bread, and the ecclesial body of the church. Reflecting on de Lubac's book, the theologian Michel de Certeau writes that the unity of these three bodies is made possible by the absence of the first. "Christianity was founded upon *the loss of a body*": we no longer have access to the body of Jesus of Nazareth, and the withdrawal of his body from history gives rise to the church and the Eucharist as "the effects of and substitutes for that absence." Jesus's body disappears, and in the void where he once was the church and its sacraments arise. Thus, for Certeau, Christian faith is "an impossible mourning," impossible because it can never be finished—we forever grieve the irrevocable absence of Jesus, and each time we gather together and break bread we bear that grief forward into a new day.[20]

20. Michel de Certeau, *The Mystic Fable, Volume I: The Sixteenth and Seventeenth Centuries*, trans. Michael B. Smith (Chicago: University of Chicago Press, 1995), 1:81–82.

Hadewijch goes further than this. It's not just that church and sacrament are "substitutes" for the lost body of Jesus. If Jesus is the incarnation of the God who is love, and if this love (as *Minne*) is a longing that goes unsated, then the sacrament gives us the real presence of Christ precisely by making present his absence and thereby kindling our longing for one who is not there. *Minne* can only be "present" in the lack and absence that stir a greater craving. In Hadewijch's eucharistic theology, the sacrament "feeds" us not by filling us with divine presence but by deepening our hunger. This paradox tangles language into knots, so Hadewijch writes poetry:

> They who live thus in hunger for Love
> And yet lack fruition,
> O who can praise them enough?
> For they as one cleave wholly to Love;
> And instead of receiving everything from her,
> They are robbed of everything . . .[21]

When it comes to the body of Christ, to be robbed of everything is already to have. The Eucharist offers a

---

21. Hadewijch, "Poem in Stanzas 15," in *The Complete Works*, 166.

taste of divine presence that is none other than living in hunger in the wake of divine absence.

This is why, in her most searing poem, Hadewijch declares that the highest name of Love—of *Minne*, of God—is Hell:

Hell is the seventh name
Of this Love wherein I suffer . . .
As Hell turns everything to ruin,
In Love nothing else is acquired
But disquiet and torture without pity;
Forever to be in unrest,
Forever assault and new persecution;
To be wholly devoured and engulfed
In her unfathomable essence,
To founder unceasingly in heat and cold,
In the deep, insurmountable darkness of Love.
This outdoes the torments of hell . . .
. . . Hell should be the highest name of Love.[22]

If the love of God brings not satisfaction and rest but craving without end, if to taste *Minne* is to die of hunger in the absence of the beloved, if God's love is longing, then the highest name of love is mysteriously the name of greatest separation from God: Hell. These

22. Hadewijch, "Poem in Couplets 16," in *The Complete Works,* 356–57.

are threads that will later be picked up by Adrienne von Speyr and Hans Urs von Balthasar: love reaches across the distance between lover and beloved, and so God's infinite love reaches across an infinite distance from God. Hell is for Hadewijch the highest name of *Minne* because it names that infinite distance across which God's love infinitely reaches. God is present where God seems most utterly absent, because the love that God only is is a hunger that cannot be filled.

I don't know how many times I read this poem during that long involuntary eucharistic fast, and I return to it still when I think of the churches I've attended with empty pews and choirs now used for storage. Hadewijch herself seems to have known such grief. Though we know almost nothing of her life, her letters hint at some rupture in her community. It seems as though she was once cherished as a leader but was then cast out. "Grieve for my sake as little as you can," she writes to a friend. "What happens to me, whether I am wandering in the country or put in prison—however it turns out, it is the work of love."[23] Some scholars speculate that she lived the rest of her life homeless, wandering, perhaps scratching her poems in the corner of a leprosarium, surrounded by other castaways.[24] Whether she was

23. Hadewijch, "Letter 29," in *The Complete Works,* 114.
24. Hadewijch, "Introduction," in *The Complete Works,* 5.

literally expelled from her community or the anguished descriptions of abandonment and loneliness are literary devices meant to illustrate her mystical theology, Hadewijch's version of Christian life is one in which exile, dispossession, and powerlessness are not humiliations from which Christians must protect ourselves at all costs. They are instead paths into a deeper communion with the God who is *Minne*, the God who is forever not here but elsewhere.

∽

What if we saw our hunger for the church, the body of Christ, not as something to be filled, but as a way of being pulled into the void of God's own hunger? What if we approached the prospect of losing the body of Christ—not just the body of Jesus, which we have always already lost, but the churches we belong to and the eucharistic ritual whose steady drumbeat has measured our lives week by week—from within Hadewijch's theology of mourning? What if, instead of insisting on prolonging the existence of recognizable forms of Christian community, we saw our mourning over their disappearance as itself the longing love that is *Minne*?

We might then, like Hadewijch, suffer from this mourning. We might be wounded by the loss of familiarity and security, by the absence of assurance that our beloved communities will outlive us. But we also might, like Hadewijch, touch in the depths of our mourning the depths of God's own mourning love.

Whatever happens, however it turns out, it is the work of love.

CHAPTER 4

Angela of Foligno
Christ on the Outside

There's an interesting rhetorical tick you'll notice among the Christian West's self-styled defenders, if you pay close enough attention. Viktor Orbán, the prime minister of Hungary and beloved statesman of the postliberal right, described in a 2022 speech "the great historic battle that we are fighting: demography, migration, gender." Trans people, immigrants, and those who threatened to make Hungary (as he put it) a "mixed-race" country blur into one single enemy, one single battle.[1]

Geert Wilders, leader of the Dutch Party for Freedom, released in 2016 a plan for the "de-Islamization" of the Netherlands. Point one of the plan was to close

1. Viktor Orbán, "Speech by Prime Minister Viktor Orbán at the 31st Bálványos Summer Free University and Student Camp" (Tusnádfürdő, July 23, 2022), https://2015-2022.miniszterelnok. hu/speech-by-prime-minister-viktor-orban-at-the-31st-balvan-yos-summer-free-university-and-student-camp/.

all mosques and ban the Quran. Point seven: No more money for wind turbines.[2] Climate activism and Muslims: one single enemy.

Jordan Peterson, the right-wing masculinity influencer, said in an interview in 2018 that "Most of the global warming posturing is a masquerade for anti-capitalists to have a go at the Western patriarchy."[3] Feminists, Marxists, and climate activists: one single enemy.

In the pall of the Christian West's twilight, outsiders lose their edges and blur together. They come to form one single existential threat, one seething undifferentiated *them* always threatening to swamp a fragile and endangered *us*. Whenever I see this bizarre blurring happening, I think of a woman from thirteenth-century Italy and her strange, disturbing, politically explosive work of mystical theology, *The Book of the Blessed Angela of Foligno*.

∞

2. Andreas Malm and the Zetkin Collective, *White Skin, Black Fuel: On the Danger of Fossil Fascism* (New York: Verso, 2021), 89.

3. Greg Callaghan, "Right-Winger? Not Me, Says Alt-Right Darling Jordan Peterson," *Sydney Morning Herald,* April 20, 2018, https://www.smh.com.au/world/north-america/right-winger-not-me-says-alt-right-darling-jordan-peterson-20180 417-p4za14.html.

The Book of the Blessed Angela of Foligno is maybe the weirdest book in the history of theology. Dictated by Angela herself, and written down by the plucky scribe Brother A. (who constantly interrupts the narrative to record his own reactions), the *Book* narrates a desire for God so all-consuming it's almost frightening.

Angela recalls visions where she yearns for God so intensely every joint in her body dislocates. She prays to feel closer to Jesus's suffering by being crucified in a sewer or being paraded naked through the town square draped in rotten meat and shrieking out her sins. And in the book's weirdest episode, she eats a piece of decomposing flesh that fell off of a leper's hand and calls it Holy Communion.

It's this last story that makes Angela's strange book one of the most politically important works of theology in Christian history, and it's this story I think of whenever I hear people propose to wall off a properly Christian society from an ill-defined and ever-threatening *them* seeking to destroy it.

∞

In 1292, on Maundy Thursday, Angela left the walled city of Foligno and traveled to the leprosarium of San Lazzaro di Corsiano—a leprosarium not unlike the ones in which Hadewijch might have spent a night.[4] "Perhaps," Angela said to a friend that morning, "we will be able to find Christ there among the poor, the suffering, and the afflicted."[5] The two women took the lepers fish and bread, ate with them, and afterward washed their hands and feet.

When she later recalled the story to Brother A., Angela mentioned one particular man. His hands "were festering and in an advanced stage of decomposition." As they washed him, pieces of his rotting body fell off and floated in the bowl of water. The women finished their work, took the bowl, and drank it. A piece of his flesh got stuck in Angela's throat, but after some effort she swallowed it down. "The drink was so sweet," she remembered; "it was as if we had received Holy Communion."[6]

As we'll see, this story is more than simply a story about a saint having compassion for the sick; it's a story about Angela looking for Christ by turning away from her self-proclaimed Christian society and toward those that society has excluded. The leper in medieval Christendom was less a medical category than a category

4. Angela of Foligno, "The *Memorial*: The Stages of Angela's Inner Journey," in *Complete Works*, trans. Paul Lachance (New York: Paulist Press, 1993), 373 n. 55. All citations from Angela's *Complete Works* are from "The *Memorial*."
    5. Angela of Foligno, *Complete Works*, 162.
    6. Angela of Foligno, *Complete Works*, 163.

of exclusion, the vague *them* against which Christian society's *us* was defined. Angela's mystical theology of mourning declares that wherever a line is drawn or a wall is built to keep a godly and pious *us* safe from a degenerate and godless *them,* the God who is forever *not here* is forever to be sought on the far side.

ॐ

Like Hadewijch, Angela's theology is marked by her excessive, forever-unsatisfied desire for God. In one vision, Angela describes aching for God and begging "that he give her something of himself." She then sees God's love "gently advancing toward her. She saw the beginning of it but not the end, only its continuation." As God's infinite love reached out for her, Angela says it moved "like a sickle": "as it approached her, love at first drew back, not bestowing itself as much as it had led her to understand it would . . . and this made her languish for more."[7]

Here she sounds as much like Weil as like Hadewijch: the advance of love is none other than withdrawal, because what advances *is* withdrawal; what is present is the lack that kindles deeper desire. "If here on earth you were granted everything you desired," God tells Angela, "you would no longer hunger for me; for

7. Angela of Foligno, *Complete Works*, 182–83.

precisely this reason, I do not want to grant your wish; for in this life, I want you to hunger for me, desire me, and languish for me."[8] Angela's love for God is a longing for one who is absent, an endless desire that drives her to seek God always *not here*, always elsewhere. Eventually, this perpetual nonsatisfaction will drive her to transgress the borders of Christendom.

Unsatisfied desire is so crucial to Angela's theology because, also like Hadewijch, she understands her relationship to God as a kind of mourning. Just before telling Brother A. of her visit to the leprosarium, Angela tells him a strange parable, weaving together the threads of longing, grief, and communal dissolution that will come to a head in her story of the leper.

Once upon a time, Angela says, there was a family whose father was wrongly executed. Long after he died, the site of his execution, "a sort of intersection of three roads," remained forever soaked in his blood. For the rest of their lives his children never ceased from mourning. They wandered the world, at times furtively passing by that same cruciform intersection, glancing at the blood-soaked ground, glancing at each other, only to be wounded again by their grief, turning away in sorrow and wandering on, each treading their own lonely path.[9]

This bleak parable of loss and exile illustrates for

8. Angela of Foligno, *Complete Works*, 152–53.
9. Angela of Foligno, *Complete Works*, 161.

Angela both Christian faith and Christian community. "Grieve and lament, O soul, which must pass by
the cross on which Christ died." The "legitimate sons of
God," as she puts it, are those who never stop mourning
the loss of Jesus and who carry that grief always in their
hearts, sorrowful wanderers cast out into the world.[10]

At this point, Brother A. stops the narrative like a
record scratch. This is all too much for him. This image
of faith as endless, furtive mourning is too "bitter." But
Angela holds her ground, insisting that her theology of
mourning is in fact "sweet."[11] To prove her point, and to
better illustrate what this mystic mourning looks like
in practice, she recalls her "Holy Communion" at the
leprosarium.

Shocking as the story might seem at first, eating
filth was kind of a trend among medieval Italian saints.
Francis of Assisi, Catherine of Siena, and Catherine of
Genoa are all said to have eaten scabs, pus, lice, or other
bodily filth. But there's something a bit different about
Angela's story, as medievalist Molly Morrison points
out. In all the other stories about filth-eating saints, the
narrative begins with the saint first being disgusted by
the suffering body of the sick person. God then chastises
them for this unkind reaction and commands them to
eat filth from the other's body as a way to overcome

10. Angela of Foligno, *Complete Works*, 161–62.
11. Angela of Foligno, *Complete Works*, 162.

their revulsion. Drawing near in love to one whom they had initially despised, the saint learns that God's love is greater than they initially thought, that God loves even this person. But Angela never mentions feeling revulsion. She has no disgust to overcome, no lesson to learn. She knows from the start that those confined in the leprosarium are beloved of God; the narrative begins with her saying she's going there to "find Christ." And all she has to say about her afternoon with the lepers is that it was "sweet." What's more, instead of describing the bits and pieces of the leper's broken body as disgusting or unclean, she compares them to the holiest thing imaginable for an Umbrian Franciscan: the consecrated bread of the Eucharist, the bits and pieces of the broken body of Christ. Morrison describes Angela's story as outlining a radical eucharistic aesthetic, in which "filth is holy, perversion is beauty."[12]

But there's something even more important happening here. Angela, after all, doesn't describe the man's wounded body as "filth," and she doesn't describe her act as "perversion." She doesn't dwell on the man's symptoms, only mentioning them to explain how the piece of his flesh came to float in the bowl of water. Her

12. Molly Morrison, "Ingesting Bodily Filth: Defilement in the Spirituality of Angela of Foligno," *Romance Quarterly* 50, no. 3 (January 2003): 207, https://doi.org/10.1080/08831150309601978.

story outlines a radical eucharistic *politics*, one that forms a vital counterweight to any political theology of power and purity. Angela doesn't dwell on the man's symptoms because his actual sickness doesn't have anything to do with the story. What matters isn't *why* the people in the leprosarium have been excluded. What matters is the bare fact of their exclusion.

∽

Leprosy was not a well-defined category in medieval Europe. There was no single disease called leprosy; instead the term named a wide variety of skin conditions. And according to historian R. I. Moore, "the leper" shouldn't even be thought of as a medical category at all. It was above all a category of social exclusion.[13]

We might expect medieval Christendom to be marked by tenderness toward lepers, owing to the many Gospel stories where Jesus seeks out lepers and shows compassion for them. These stories linger on Jesus's longing to draw near the lepers, carefully narrating how he "stretched out his hand" toward them. In Europe from the tenth through the thirteenth century, however, lepers were ruthlessly driven out of town and

13. R. I. Moore, *The Formation of a Persecuting Society: Authority and Deviance in Western Europe, 950–1250* (Malden, MA: Blackwell Publishing, 2007).

kept away, subjected to a strict regime of surveillance, segregation, and deportation.

And they weren't the only ones. Recall that this is the same time period studied by Henri de Lubac and Simone Weil, when Western Christendom was constructing itself as a bounded and homogenous *corpus mysticum* modeled on the pure white host of the *corpus verum*. And this self-construction happened through the exclusion of various categories of people: the leper, the Jew, the heretic, the "sodomite."[14] These different excluded groups were subjected to the same indignities: forced to wear special clothing identifying them as outsiders, herded into ghettoes, barred from holding public office, their property expropriated, shunned from associating with accepted members of the social body. And through suffering these same indignities they eventually stopped being, in the eyes of Christendom, different groups, becoming instead one amorphous *them*—one single enemy—against which a Christian society could become a coherent *us*.

As the same practices of exclusion were brought down on these various groups, the same paranoid conspiracies swirled around them. Jews were periodically accused of poisoning wells as a justification for Chris-

14. For the history of the concept of sodomy in medieval theology, see Mark D. Jordan, *The Invention of Sodomy in Christian Theology* (Chicago: University of Chicago Press, 1997).

tians killing them and stealing their property, and so too in the early fourteenth century the French inquisition tortured a group of lepers, forced them to confess they had poisoned wells all over the country, and then burned them and seized the leprosarium's assets. There was even a rumor in 1321 that Jews and lepers were working together in a grand conspiracy to exterminate all of France's Christians.[15]

The various categories of exclusion blended together into one single threat: heresy was imagined as a sexually transmitted disease, just like leprosy; a symptom of both was a kind of hypersexuality at times leading to same-sex relations; hypersexuality was considered a Jewish trait; Judaism was considered a heresy; Jews, lepers, heretics, and sodomites met with the devil at night to plot the destruction of Christendom. All of these categories of exclusion, Moore argues, were interchangeable, and their persecutions can't be considered independently of each other.

These persecutions had a long afterlife. In Brittany, the area of northwest France where my grandmother lived until fleeing the Nazi invasion, there was into the twentieth century a persecuted underclass known as Caquins, or Cagots.[16] No one knows why they were per-

15. Moore, *The Formation of a Persecuting Society*, 60.
16. Shelby T. McCloy, "The Cagots: A Despised People in France," *South Atlantic Quarterly* 54, no. 1 (January 1, 1955):

secuted or when it started. Nothing about their appearance or way of speaking set them apart from other Bretons. The only thing distinct about Caquins was the persecution itself. They were forbidden to marry non-Caquins; they had their own cemeteries and their own segregated sections of churches; they had to wear special badges; in parish birth records their names were written upside down; they had to be baptized at night and in silence. By the time the discrimination was written into law, well into the 1400s, whatever might have started it all was long forgotten.

So the Bretons invented reasons. They claimed Caquins were descended from some other despised group. Some said their ancestors were lepers. Others, heretics. Others, Jews. What's the difference? As Moore writes, in the medieval imagination, lepers, heretics, and Jews "had the same qualities, from the same source, and they presented the same threat": the end of Christian civilization.[17]

The leper, then, was not a medical category but a structural one. I expect this is why Angela doesn't dwell on how the leper's symptoms made her feel. Whatever actual disease he had is beside the point. She's more interested in his structural position as the one who is

44–55, https://doi.org/10.1215/00382876-54-1-44.
    17. Moore, *The Formation of a Persecuting Society*, 61.

excluded. The leper, like the Jew, the heretic, and the sodomite, functioned as what Judith Butler calls "the constitutive outside."[18] Every community is defined in part by all the communities it is not. There's nothing inherently violent about this. After all, difference is the ground of love, desire, and solidarity. We can, like Jesus, stretch out our hand. But when one's own community is understood as a privileged site of goodness and holiness, or an ever-threatened site of security and prosperity, exclusion becomes deadly. This is what happened to lepers in medieval Christendom. Imagined as the outside that always lurked threateningly inside the *corpus mysticum*, they were routinely surveilled, arrested, deported, segregated, and killed. And it's here, among Christendom's constitutive outside, that Angela seeks Christ.

❧

We no longer drive out from our towns lepers and heretics. But there are plenty of groups today whose exclusion is imagined as necessary to secure a Christian society. In 2024, at the Republican National Convention, attendees celebrated the party's promise to "keep foreign Christian-hating Communists, Marxists, and Socialists out of America," while waving signs reading "MASS DEPOR-

18. Judith Butler, *Bodies That Matter: On the Discursive Limits of "Sex"* (New York: Routledge, 1993), 52–53.

TATION NOW!"[19] A few months later, the party swept control of the federal government. At home and abroad, political movements wrapping themselves in the mantle of defending Christianity require the violent exclusion of *them* to maintain a coherent *us*. And just as in Angela's day, today the various figures who fill the role of that *them* blur together into one existential threat—as in Viktor Orbán's speech against "demography, migration, gender," or Geert Wilders's plan to "De-Islamize" the Netherlands by getting rid of wind turbines.

The blurring can become so absurd it would be funny if the consequences weren't so deadly. American right-wing politicians spread rumors of Muslim prayer rugs and "military-age Chinese males" found at the Mexican border; white nationalists describe gender-affirming healthcare and immigration as two prongs of a plan by Jewish elites to drive down white birthrates; French politicians warn that gender studies departments are the vanguard of "Islamo-leftism." The fantasy that trans children, ISIS, Chinese communist secret agents, Honduran refugees, and climate activists are merely different faces of one single assault on Christian society is as ridiculous as the fantasy that Jews and lepers were meeting in secret to poison all the wells in

19. "2024 Republican Party Platform," The American Presidency Project, July 8, 2024, https://www.presidency.ucsb.edu/documents/2024-republican-party-platform.

France. But fantasies follow their own logic. A coherent *us* requires the exclusion of *them*, no matter how incoherent that *them* is.

༃

Seeking Jesus among Christian society's constitutive outside, Angela's journey to the leper colony points to how a theology of mourning might be lived today. The theologian Michel de Certeau defines the "mystic," which Angela surely was, as one who "cannot stop walking and, with the certainty of what is lacking, knows of every place and object that it is *not that*; one cannot stay *there* nor be content with *that*."[20] The mystic is a mourner, reaching out for one who is forever absent yet in their reaching brushing up against the world. Angela's mystic mourning—her vision of faith as grief, wandering, and endless desire—has a sharply political edge. Her fathomless desire led her away from the self-proclaimed godliness of her Christian community and toward those deemed ungodly, away from Christendom's *us* and toward its *them*.

The God whose love moves like a sickle, whose approach is withdrawal and whose presence is absence, is a God sought always elsewhere, always on the other side of any wall that a so-called Christian society might

20. Certeau, *The Mystic Fable,* 1:299.

build around itself. Beyond any politics of mere tolerance or inclusion—which demands the assimilation of every difference to a universal *us*—Angela's theology acknowledges that there is always an outside to any Christian community and yet insists that Christ is to be sought on the other side of wherever we draw that line. "Boundaries are the place of the Christian work," Certeau writes elsewhere, "and their displacements are the result of this work."[21]

Angela's boundary-displacing theology has inspired antifascist resistance before. I first read about her *Book* in the diaries kept during World War II by the French antifascist writer Georges Bataille. Sick with tuberculosis and unable to fight, Bataille spent the war years in a cottage in Nazi-occupied rural France while a Jewish couple hid in his Paris apartment. His diary opens on September 5, 1939—two days after France declared war on Germany. "I begin because of events," he writes, "but not to speak of them." He speaks instead of "standing on a crowded train . . . reading Angela of Foligno's *Book of Visions*."[22]

21. Michel de Certeau, "How Is Christianity Thinkable Today?," in *The Postmodern God: A Theological Reader*, ed. Graham Ward; trans. Frederick Christian Bauerschmidt and Catriona Hanley (Malden, MA: Blackwell Publishers, 1997), 142–55, 151.

22. Georges Bataille, *Guilty*, trans. Stuart Kendall (Albany: State University of New York Press, 2011), 9.

Bataille had long understood fascism as grounded in Christian theology, and he saw a possible theological ground for resistance in Angela's excessive desire and attention to the abject and the excluded. "I am copying, unable to say how excited I am: the veil is torn, I'm coming out of the fog of my thrashing impotence."[23] His diary became a chronicle of his own excessive mysticism, as he sought to resist fascism's political theology through a counter-political theology of tragedy and vulnerability.

The Memorial of the Blessed Angela of Foligno remains as politically radical in our day as it was in Bataille's—and in her own. The categories of people whose exclusion makes possible the fantasy of a unified Christendom shift over time. Once it was lepers and heretics and sodomites. For today's defenders of the Christian West it is refugees and trans people and Muslims. Tomorrow there will be new categories of exclusion. Angela teaches us that however these walls get built, wherever these lines get drawn, our yearning for a God who is always *not here* should lead us to transgress them, to turn away from an imagined *us* and toward those excluded and demeaned for their unassimilable difference.

23. Bataille, *Guilty*, 9.

PART 3

Resurrection

London, 1943

She wasn't supposed to be here. Stuck in this cramped office, looking through the slit window at the gray-on-gray of London. She should have been standing at the open door of an airplane, the gouged and smoldering French countryside at her back, smoke whipping past her unkempt hair, locking eyes with her circle of chosen women. Matching white uniforms, parachutes strapped to their backs, counting down from ten, ready for death. She could see it so clearly it hurt. The rage felt like it was clawing out her insides; but her pen glided steadily, and when she hit the bottom of the page her free hand added it to the pile and put a new one beneath the moving pen, all in one fluid motion. Simone Weil sat surrounded by piles and piles of paper written in her perfect handwriting, but in her mind she was parachuting onto the front lines; she was binding up the maimed leg of a Resistance fighter; she was giving her canteen to a gutshot Wehrmacht soldier; she was tied to a chair in a farmhouse

*basement as a Gestapo agent pulled out her fingernails.
She was anywhere but here.*

*Weil reminded herself how she got here. When the
Germans began making their way south to Marseilles,
she had no choice but to get her parents on that ship to
New York. And she had to leave New York for London
if there was any hope of meeting the Resistance lead-
ership and presenting them her plan for an elite corps
of parachuting frontline nurses. Much like Henri de
Lubac, Weil understood the war as a fundamentally
theological struggle, a grand contest between two con-
cepts of the mystical body. On the one hand, there was
the fascist body politic, the mystical expression of the
idealized Aryan body, purifying itself of all undesirable
members and concentrating all its power into the sum-
mit of the Führer's sovereign will. The perfect instantia-
tion of the fascist mystical body was the SS: handpicked
for their beauty and racial purity, inducted in dramatic
torchlit ceremonies, parachuting onto the battlefield in
their dashing uniforms, tasked with the cruelest acts of
enslavement and mass killing, counting their lives as
nothing against the destiny of the Volk. They were the
fascist* corpus mysticum *in miniature, and the Allies
needed to confront them with an antifascist* corpus
mysticum *of their own.*

*Weil saw her nurses' corps as a direct rebuke of the SS:
handpicked from the childless adult women so scorned*

by fascists everywhere, inducted in the quotidian selfless-ness of CPR classes, parachuting onto the battlefield to carry out acts of indiscriminate care, counting their lives as nothing for the sake of lessening others' suffering.

She presented her plan to everyone she knew with any connections to the Free French forces. They all laughed at her. Eventually she went to London to show the plan to Charles de Gaulle himself. "She's crazy!" he spat. But she wouldn't go away; so they stuck her in an office and gave her the make-work job of writing up a plan for a new con-stitution once the Nazis were driven out of France. That would keep her busy. So there she sat, ignored, belittled, scratching away with her pen day and night, writing what would become her masterpiece: The Need for Roots.

꩜

The Need for Roots was supposed to be a blueprint for how the French government could be rebuilt after five years of fascist occupation. Weil had a reputation as a brilliant and eclectic young political philosopher, decidedly on the left yet harshly critical of the commu-nists and willing to fold in ideas from the right. The Free French, to the extent they thought of Weil at all as she sat hunched over her desk, probably imagined a treatise on national renewal that would have been pal-atable to the patchwork coalition of the Resistance.

The need to drive out the Nazi invaders had brought together anarchists and nationalists, communists and business leaders, social democrats and far-rightists. This couldn't last. The Free French hoped for a fresh vision of the nation that would avoid a civil war starting up as soon as the Nazis left, and Weil's political weirdness made her a good candidate for imagining a restored France that might hold everyone together. But for Weil, it was exactly this idea that Nazism was a foreign contagion, this fantasy of a pure France uncontaminated by fascism lying buried and waiting to be dusted off, that had to be dismantled if there was ever going to be something like a "France after fascism."

Allied propaganda often depicted Nazi Germany as a horde of heathen barbarians besieging a noble Christian civilization. *The Need for Roots* attacks this fantasy directly, arguing that fascism grew from the soil of the Christian West. This is the text in which she declared that the West's "conception of greatness is the same one which has inspired Hitler's whole life."[1]

In the fascist imagination, it's great to dominate; it's great to bend the world to your will; it's great to be remembered long after your death as someone who turned the wheel of history. Those in the Allied countries might look on in horror as the Nazis conquered

1. Weil, *The Need for Roots*, 217.

Eastern Europe, but as soon as they turned their eyes
to their own countries and their own pasts—their glorious colonial adventures in Africa and Indochina,
their great men of history like Cardinal Richelieu and
George Washington, the romance of the old plantation
and the open frontier—they too agreed that it's great
to rule; it's great to command. That's why, for Weil, a
military defeat of fascism wouldn't be enough. As long
as the West kept its idea that greatness means exercising
power over others, it was going to keep getting roiled
by movements striving for new heights of this kind of
greatness. What is needed, *The Need for Roots* argues,
is a new conception of greatness, one so utterly transformed that no one would ever think to describe Hitler
as a great man.

For Weil, our false conception of greatness is buried at the heart of the Christian West; so transforming
greatness requires a profound transformation of Christian theology. We've seen already how she reimagined
the story of creation. But for her, the theological concept most to blame for our false conception of greatness
is that of Jesus's resurrection. Rather than reimagine
resurrection, though, she tried to discard it entirely.

The more Weil wandered in precarious exile after
fleeing Paris in 1940, the more deeply she drew from
Christian theology. But the resurrection never interested her. "The Cross by itself suffices me," she wrote in

a letter explaining why she would never officially convert to Christianity.[2] She was above all enamored with Paul's claim in Philippians that God, as Weil summarized it, "stripped himself of divinity."[3]

Creation, incarnation, crucifixion, and Eucharist were for her one deepening movement of self-stripping and effacement. God became less so the world could arise, then became even less in being born an ordinary human being, then even less by being made into a corpse, then even less by emptying into the bare matter of bread and wine. She believed that to say Jesus rose from the dead is to reverse this movement of withdrawal, to restore the loss, and so she was never able to say it. "Today," she wrote, "the glorious Christ veils from us the one who was made a malediction," and "the degradation which is the very essence of the Passion is hardly felt by us."[4] Weil saw the resurrection stories as evidence of a deep-seated inability to mourn the death of Jesus. And, like Freud, she saw this revolt against mourning as politically dangerous.

By the time she wrote *The Need for Roots*, Weil would see resurrection theology as central to the false

2. Simone Weil, *Letter to a Priest*, trans. Arthur Wills (New York: Penguin Books, 2003), 55.

3. Weil, *Notebooks*, 284.

4. Weil, *Intimations of Christianity among the Ancient Greeks*, 142–43.

conception of greatness that led the Christian West to give itself over to fascism. The first Christians, she wrote, were unable to see Christ on the cross, the Christ who so completely refused to exercise force that he was willing to be killed and used his last breath to forgive his killers, as the "absolutely pure being" he was. They needed some display of power to prove his greatness, and so they told each other that he had risen from the dead "and was to return before very long in his glory to recompense his own and punish all the rest."[5]

Thus, from almost the very beginning, Christians imagined Jesus as an omnipotent sovereign rewarding friends and punishing enemies. They imagined Jesus, in other words, as a Roman emperor on a cosmic scale, master even of life and death. This is "the Roman conception of God," Weil wrote in *The Need for Roots*, and through this conception "the Roman spirit of imperialism and domination" infected nearly the whole of the Christian West.[6] Nazi Germany, for her, was simply the purest expression of this Roman worship of force.[7]

5. Weil, *The Need for Roots*, 218.

6. Weil, *The Need for Roots*, 276.

7. See her lengthy comparison of Nazi and Roman policy in Simone Weil, "The Great Beast: Some Reflections on the Origins of Hitlerism," in *Selected Essays, 1934–1943: Historical, Political, and Moral Writings*, trans. Richard Rees (Eugene, OR: Wipf & Stock Publishers, 2015), 89–144.

To truly defeat fascism, the Christian West would have to completely transform its conception of greatness, which for Weil required renouncing the idea that Jesus did not die an ordinary death like any other human being but conquered death and rose in glory to sit upon an everlasting throne and rule a subjected universe. She called for a Christianity beyond resurrection, a Christianity in which the cross suffices. To defeat fascism, she insisted, Christians must learn to truly mourn the death of Jesus.

∽

Weil's reasons for rejecting the resurrection are compelling. Instead of giving scientistic reasons for not believing, she gives theological ones. God refuses to exercise power over creation, so any talk of God "conquering" or "defeating" death in a moment of glory must not be true. The love that is God is a movement of continuous withdrawal, so to say the loss of Jesus was reversed and his presence restored must also miss the mark. The incarnation is God taking on human finitude and pronouncing it good; so to say Jesus did not die an ordinary human death undercuts that incarnational claim. Weil rejects the resurrection not because she thinks it's inconsistent with how the world works, but because she thinks it's inconsistent with how God works. The cross by itself should suffice.

While Weil's reasons are convincing, I'm not convinced those reasons necessarily lead to her conclusion. That is, she rejects a wrong idea of the resurrection for right reasons. What if there were a better way to think of the resurrection, one entirely compatible with her theology of absence and mourning? If she's right that the struggle against fascism must be waged on theology's ground, then that struggle is best waged not by jettisoning the resurrection but by thinking about it differently. Rather than viewing resurrection as a reversal of God's self-effacing act, and thus as the overcoming of our mourning for Jesus's death, what if resurrection were understood as the continuation of that self-effacement and thus the deepening of our mourning? That Jesus is risen would be not the end of our grief but its beginning.

᠀

This final section of this book traces a theology of resurrection that meets Weil's challenge and contributes to her effort to wholly transform our conception of greatness. Where Christian theology has often imagined Jesus's resurrection as the restoration of a loss and a liberation from frailty and finitude, an act of divine power extending to us God's everlasting perfection, this section explores an alternate theology of resurrection in which the resurrection of Jesus is instead a way of naming the unending work of mourning his loss.

In chapter 5, we will dig deep into the roots of Christian history, following recent scholarship in New Testament and early Christian studies investigating the tantalizing hints into what Christian community between Jesus's death and the first written Gospels may have looked like. In the mourning rituals performed by women in Hellenistic Palestine, songs were sung and meals were shared at the gravesites of lost loves; and it was believed that the dead's own voice reverberated in the singing of the mourners, and the dead's hunger was met in meeting the hunger of the bereaved.

According to some groundbreaking work by feminist scholars, these ancient women's mourning rituals may have been the first stirrings of both our resurrection faith that Jesus could be met again on the far side of his death and our eucharistic faith that he is present in the meals shared in his memory. The chapter builds on this suggestive research, putting it in conversation with twentieth-century antifascist worries about the political dangers of resurrection theology, to argue that we encounter the resurrected Jesus not when our longing for him is satisfied but in the longing stirred by his ever-unfilled absence.

Chapter 6 explores the political implications of this understanding of resurrection through a reading of the French Jesuit Michel de Certeau. Certeau wrote a handful of theological essays at the turn of the 1970s, when he felt Christianity in the Western world was on the brink of disappearing. He was not alone in thinking this way. At that same time, also in France, a conservative Catholic travel writer named Jean Raspail felt himself living through the end of the Christian West. Raspail wrote a novel, *The Camp of the Saints*, in which he urged what remained of the Christian West to defend itself with lethal force against transformation and disappearance.

Today, *The Camp of the Saints* is celebrated by the pundits and politicians of the radical right as a "prophetic" work predicting the demise of Western Christian civilization. Chapter 6 presents Certeau as an altogether different kind of "prophet" and guide through the twilight of the Christian West. Rather than succumbing to rage and violence, Certeau faces the dissolution of familiar cultural forms from the perspective of resurrection faith grounded in the emptiness of the tomb. As the angel said to the women: "He is not here; he has gone to Galilee." The Christ of the empty tomb is never here but always elsewhere—never within the familiar and expected site of a "Christian culture" but always waiting to be encountered in the struggles and needs of those beyond it.

CHAPTER 5

Resurrection as Mourning

Passover, year 70. Roman troops encircled Jerusalem. The city was full of Jewish travelers from all over the known world. Now they were trapped. The emperor Titus, encamped with his troops, brought with him a translator: Flavius Josephus, a former Judean general who had surrendered and defected. Years later, Josephus recalled the five months of siege. Food supplies in Jerusalem quickly ran out and the city descended into chaos and civil war. "Children pulled the very morsels that their fathers were eating out of their very mouths," Josephus wrote, "and what was still more to be pitied, so did the mothers do as to their infants."[1] Gangs broke into homes to murder the inhabitants and steal what handfuls of grain they hoarded. Rumors swirled that some were betraying the city to the Romans in exchange for food, and makeshift tribunals tortured and executed the accused traitors.

---

1. Flavius Josephus, "The Wars of the Jews," in *The Works of Flavius Josephus*, trans. William Whiston (Halifax: William Milner, 1849), book V, line 430 (p. 587).

Those who snuck outside the walls looking for grass to fill their empty stomachs were captured by Roman soldiers. "They were first whipped," Josephus observed, "and then tormented with all sorts of tortures, before they died, and were then crucified before the wall of the city." Josephus estimated that five hundred Jews were crucified every day. "So the soldiers, out of the wrath and hatred they bore the Jews, nailed those they caught, one after one way, and another after another, to the crosses, by way of jest." The area just outside the walls filled with mangled and twisted corpses, until "room was wanting for the crosses, and crosses wanting for the bodies."[2]

The siege lasted for months. By the end, famine had "devoured the people by whole houses and families; the upper rooms were full of women and children that were dying by famine, and the lanes of the city were full of the dead bodies of the aged." Those who lingered on were too weakened by starvation even to sing the traditional mourning songs for the dead. "A deep silence also, and a kind of deadly night, had seized upon the city."[3] People ate shoes, leather straps, clothing. People ate their own children. Eventually the Romans moved into the city and burned the Temple to the ground. They

2. Josephus, "The Wars," book V, lines 449–51 (p. 588).
3. Josephus, "The Wars," book V, lines 512–15 (p. 591).

rampaged through Jerusalem killing the survivors and enslaving what few women and children remained. By Josephus's estimate, 1.1 million Jews died during the siege and 97,000 survivors were enslaved, either to be worked to death in the mines or murdered for entertainment in the theaters.

A few years after the siege, a survivor of the war wrote down the story of the life and death of Jesus of Nazareth.[4] In the wake of the destruction of Jerusalem, after its smoldering streets were lined with thousands of scourged and crucified corpses, the Gospel of Mark tells a story of God incarnate as yet one more scourged and crucified Jewish man. God is like these, the Gospel declares, not an emperor like Titus.

The earliest surviving version of the Gospel of Mark ends with Jesus's resurrection, but without any note of triumph. A group of women arrive at the tomb to anoint Jesus's body. They find the tomb empty, except for a strange young man, who tells them "He is not here." The man instructs the women to tell their friends that Jesus has risen and gone to Galilee. But they don't.

4. I am grateful to Matthew Ichihashi Potts for first making me aware of just how much the Gospel texts must have been influenced by the siege of Jerusalem. For an argument that the author of Mark was a survivor of Rome's assault on Galilee, see Stephen Simon Kimondo, *The Gospel of Mark and the Roman-Jewish War of 66–70 CE: Jesus' Story as a Contrast to the Events of the War* (Eugene, OR: Pickwick Publications, 2018).

Instead "they went out and fled from the tomb, for terror and amazement had seized them, and they said nothing to anyone, for they were afraid" (Mark 16:8). Mark ends with these women grieving, traumatized, and silent.

The author of the Gospel of Mark, seeking a way to understand Jesus's divinity that had nothing to do with the ostentation and violence of empire, turned to women like these and their practices of mourning. According to recent feminist scholarship in New Testament and early Christian studies, the earliest written Christian theologies of resurrection, and even of the Eucharist, appear to borrow from traditional Hellenistic women's funerary rites.[5] What kept faith in Jesus

5. Kathleen Corley, *Maranatha: Women's Funerary Rituals and Christian Origins* (Minneapolis: Fortress Press, 2010); Carolyn Osiek, "The Women at the Tomb: What Are They Doing There?" *HTS Teologiese Studies/Theological Studies* 53, no. 1/2 (January 11, 1997): 103–18; Angela Standhartinger, "'What Women Were Accustomed to Do for the Dead Beloved by Them' ('Gospel of Peter' 12.50): Traces of Laments and Mourning Rituals in Early Easter, Passion, and Lord's Supper Traditions," *Journal of Biblical Literature* 129, no. 3 (2010): 559–74; Marianne Sawicki, *Seeing the Lord: Resurrection and Early Christian Practices* (Minneapolis: Fortress Press, 1994); Antoinette Clark Wire, "Rising Voices: The Resurrection Witness of New Testament Non-Writers," in *On the Cutting Edge: The Study of Women in Biblical Worlds. Essays in Honor of Elisabeth Schüssler Fiorenza*, ed. Jane Schaberg, Alice Bach, and Esther Fuchs (New York: Continuum, 2004), 221–29.

alive through the war-torn decades between the scattering of the disciples in the wake of his murder in the early 30s CE and the first texts written by nascent Christian communities in the 70s and what opened to those communities their way of imagining Jesus's divinity beyond empire's domination were the songs of lament and the funeral meals shared by scattered handfuls of grieving Palestinian women.

Yet, as Simone Weil observes, the movement that began as a refusal of empire's violence became, after a few generations, the religion of that same empire. God was imagined as relating to the world not as yet one more crucified body in a sea of crucified bodies but as an emperor magnified to a cosmic scale. Christianity became "defiled," in Weil's words, by Rome. And she blamed this defilement on the theology of the resurrection, seeing resurrection theology as a refusal to mourn the death of Jesus and a retreat into fantasies of infinite power and permanence. For Weil, the defilement of Christianity by Rome was a persistent problem, which erupted in her own time in fascism's political theology and would continue to erupt until the Christian West learned to mourn Jesus's death.

While this chapter follows Weil's critique of dominant resurrection theologies, it departs from her in offering a different theology of resurrection rather than jettisoning resurrection altogether. Following the author of Mark, we will turn to the grief rituals of ancient Palestinian women, learning from them a way to understand resurrection not as the overcoming of mourning but its deepening.[6] Often, as the theologian Donald MacKinnon observed, we speak of the resurrection as if it were "a descent from the cross postponed for thirty-six hours."[7] But there have always been other theologies of resurrection that do not draw such a hard line between resurrection and loss. This chapter will lay out such a theology, reading Jesus's resurrection in a tragic key—not as the overcoming of loss but as a way of naming the irrevocability of loss and the arduous task of carrying on in its wake. Viewing resurrection in this way, we might better resist the imperial political theology criticized by people like Weil and oppose the revolt against mourning gripping our world today.

꙳

6. This chapter focuses on the reconstruction of women's mourning rituals in Hellenistic Palestine by New Testament and early Christian scholars. For contributions and challenges to theology by present-day Palestinian women, see especially Naim S. Ateek, Marc H. Ellis, and Rosemary Radford Ruether, eds., *Faith and the Intifada: Palestinian Christian Voices* (Maryknoll, NY: Orbis Books, 1992), 119–34.

7. Donald M. MacKinnon, *Borderlands of Theology: And Other Essays* (London: Lutterworth, 1968), 95.

Simone Weil was not the only one in her time who saw a connection between the theology of resurrection and the politics of fascism. There were others, too, who thought the concept of resurrection inculcated certain psychological and social reflexes—a fear of loss and transience, a longing for permanence, an expectation that one can be saved from the anxieties of living and dying by an act of sovereign power—that culminated in the obedience of fascist subjects.[8]

The philosophers and social critics Theodor Adorno and Max Horkheimer, in their *Dialectic of Enlightenment*, wrote in that book's "Theses on Anti-Semitism" that fascism's "fanatical faith" in the leader's power to preserve the nation through violence was a secularization of a much older Christian belief that eternal self-preservation could be secured through submission to Christ as lord and master of the universe.[9] The Jewish

8. I draw here on Alexander Irwin's reading of Georges Bataille: "Bataille saw in monotheistic Christianity the historical template of centralized, hierarchical domination, thus in a sense the very root of authoritarian politics. The worship of the Christian God established a pattern that culminated in the servile adoration of the Führer. Thus, to combat fascism required killing God; not merely as a theological postulate, but on the deeper level of ingrained psychological and social reflexes." See Alexander Irwin, *Saints of the Impossible: Bataille, Weil, and the Politics of the Sacred* (Minneapolis: University of Minnesota Press, 2002), 21.

9. Max Horkheimer and Theodor W. Adorno, *Dialectic of*

writer Walter Benjamin, in his mystical "Theologico-Political Fragment," described fascism as a "political theocracy" that promised an end to transience through the building up by violence of an everlasting divine kingdom, a political theology grounded in Christianity's promise that "downfall" and loss will be recuperated and immortality secured through an act of divine power.[10] And for Georges Bataille, philosopher and erstwhile friend of Weil, the idea of Jesus's resurrection turned Christianity from what had initially been a rebellious anti-imperial sect into the fullest expression of the cult of the emperor: "Now God was nothing more than the emperor whose sacred robes he glorified on the church walls, in the same way that the emperor was, for his part, the image of God on earth."[11]

For these theologically minded antifascists, resurrection theology is politically dangerous. It teaches us that our finitude and frailty are temporary embarrassments from which God's infinite power can save us—an idea

Enlightenment: Philosophical Fragments, ed. Gunzelin Schmid Noerr; trans. Edmund Jephcott (Stanford, CA: Stanford University Press, 2002), 144.

10. Walter Benjamin, *Reflections: Essays, Aphorisms, Autobiographical Writing*, ed. Peter Demetz (New York: Schocken Books, 1986), 312–13.

11. Denis Hollier, ed., *The College of Sociology (1937–39)*, trans. Betsy Wing (Minneapolis: University of Minnesota Press, 1988), 134.

easily exploited by political powers, who present transformation, difference, and risk as exogenous threats
from which the worthy can be protected through acts
of sovereign violence. Thus Bataille insisted that resisting fascism required first cultivating what he called "the
hatred of salvation," turning against any idea of resurrection and its promise of permanence through power and
instead embracing a tragic theology of irrevocable loss.[12]

It is worth sitting with the disturbing fact that some of
the writers who saw the threat of fascism most clearly—
Bataille, Benjamin, Adorno, Weil, but also W. E. B. Du
Bois, Karl Löwith, Aimé Césaire, and others—understood fascism's patterns of authority and submission
as developments of specifically Christian patterns, and
that they frequently singled out resurrection theology
as the crucible in which these patterns were forged. We
should take these critiques of resurrection seriously.

But it is also worth asking if these writers' critiques of
resurrection are too reductive. They may hit the mark
when it comes to the most dominant voices in Christian
history, who largely do describe Jesus's resurrection
as the defeat of death by an act of omnipotent divine
force promising permanence and purity to the chosen.
But the dominant voices in a tradition are not the only

12. Georges Bataille, *Inner Experience*, trans. Leslie Anne
Boldt (Albany: State University of New York Press, 1988), 174.

voices. There run throughout Christian history other traditions, offering other ways of thinking about Jesus's resurrection. If Weil, Bataille, Adorno, and Benjamin are right that resurrection theology helped shape the political imaginary of fascism, perhaps a different theology of resurrection can shape a politics of resistance.

ॐ

Many of the antifascists who found resurrection theology politically dangerous drew on Friedrich Nietzsche's critique of Christianity. For Nietzsche, Christianity is nothing but one great revolt against mourning. When Jesus died a humiliated criminal and all the disciples' dreams of ruling at his side went up in smoke, wrote Nietzsche, the disciples scattered. They only came back together once they began telling each other that he had returned, that their grief was only temporary, and soon he would come back one last time to smash the unbelievers and finally give his followers the power they had craved for so long. "Precisely the most unevangelistic of feelings, *revengefulness,* again came uppermost," Nietzsche wrote. "The affair could not possibly be at an end with this death: one required 'retribution,' 'judgment.'" For Nietzsche, the resurrection stories mark a deep-seated refusal to mourn Jesus's death, a refusal of mourning motivated by a desire for revenge in which divine power would separate the righteous few from the condemned masses, granting immortality to *us* and laying waste to *them*.[13]

Nietzsche is an astute reader of the Gospels, but he misses how traumatized and grief-stricken the disciples remain at the end of the texts. The Gospels' post-resurrection stories aren't exactly stories in which the one who had been lost is triumphantly restored. The earliest version of Mark, after all, ends with the confusion and silence of the women who came to care for Jesus's body.

The other Gospels have more detailed resurrection stories, but here too there is no straightforward reversal of loss. In Matthew 28:9, the women meet Jesus "suddenly" after they find the tomb empty, but just as suddenly he sends them away back to Galilee, to where their story began and where the disciples have retreated in guilt and shame over their failure. Luke 24:31 writes of two disciples walking to Emmaus and meeting a stranger on the way, befriending him by telling him of their grief. When they arrive at their destination, they invite their new friend to stay, offering to shelter him from the dangers of wandering alone at night. The stranger sits down to dinner and breaks bread, and in the break-

13. Friedrich Wilhelm Nietzsche, *Twilight of the Idols: and, The Anti-Christ*, trans. R. J. Hollingdale (New York: Penguin Books, 2003), 165.

ing of the bread the disciples see in him the one they have lost—and immediately "he vanished from their sight." John gives a rich tableau of resurrection appearances. Yet in none of them is grief overcome. Mary Magdalene, weeping at the tomb, turns to a gardener to tell him of her sorrow. When the gardener speaks her name, she recognizes him as Jesus, but just as quickly he withdraws from her—"Don't touch me!"—and tells her instead to seek out the other mourners (John 29:17). In John 21:12, the final resurrection appearance has the disciples sitting down to breakfast with a stranger on the beach. Peter, who betrayed, denied, and abandoned Jesus, is told three times that he has not fallen beyond the reach of God's love (John 21:15–19). His sorrow is not undone; he is shown a way to live with it.

These stories of resurrection are not, as Nietzsche, Bataille, and Weil would have it, triumphant tales in which loss is reversed through the awesome violence of divine might. They are painful stories haunted by loss, in which a community shattered by grief finds, in the depth of their sorrow, new and unexpected possibilities for carrying on. Yet at the same time, Bataille and Weil are surely right that this mournful note has been repressed in favor of a politically dangerous theology that presents resurrection as infinite power's victory over loss.

But loss remains in the Gospels' resurrection stories. These are stories in which the absence of the beloved is held fast to, and in which this attachment to an absence opens the mourning community to the possibility of being transformed by new attachments. Resurrection, in the Gospels, is not an individual thing, something that happens *to me*; and far less is it a promise that the individual will continue to exist forever. The resurrection stories in the Gospels are about a community crushed, scattered, dead, and then the painful opening up of this community to the possibility of living on.

Far from promising permanence, Jesus's resurrection promises precisely that the communities that mourn his loss will *not* remain as they are forever. The new life to which the mourning community is opened isn't everlasting stasis and homogeneity but ceaseless differentiation, expanding possibilities for new relationships—an endless proliferation of new and unexpected communities, each finite and consigned to loss yet each in its passing giving way to something new.

The Gospels' endings tell of the formation of what Rowan Williams calls "communities of resurrection," communities made possible by the absence of Jesus.[14] Thus resurrection faith is, as the theologian Louis-Marie

14. Rowan Williams, *Resurrection: Interpreting the Easter Gospel* (New York: Pilgrim Press, 1984).

Chauvet puts it, "a permanent work of mourning."[15] Chauvet describes the resurrection as confronting us with the loss of Jesus rather than delivering us from that loss: "Now, as risen, Christ has departed; we must agree to this loss if we want to be able to find him."[16] We "find him" through the very work of mourning him, because to mourn is at once to be wounded by the death of the one we love but also, in that wounding, to be assured that the death of the beloved is not the death of love.

To grieve is to be assured that love is stronger than death. And in the unique case of Jesus, who is himself love, to continue to love him in the wake of his passing is to encounter the love that he is on the far side of his death. To mourn him is already to meet him resurrected.

֍

What might sound like a heterodox and postmodern reading of resurrection in fact has deep roots. I mentioned earlier that feminist scholars studying the origins of Christianity have argued that the Gospels'

15. Louis-Marie Chauvet, *Symbol and Sacrament: A Sacramental Reinterpretation of Christian Existence*, trans. Patrick Madigan and Madeleine Beaumont (Collegeville, MN: Liturgical Press, 1995), 74.

16. Chauvet, *Symbol and Sacrament*, 177.

resurrection narratives draw on the older and decidedly less triumphalist funerary practices of Hellenistic women. In first-century Palestine, these scholars point out, it was common for women to gather together on the third day after a death to sing stories about their lost love while sharing a meal of fish, wine, and bread. In these communal outpourings of grief, the dead beloved was felt to be present among the mourners, joining in the song and sharing in the meal. The New Testament scholar Kathleen Corley argues that the eucharistic faith that Jesus is present in the bread and wine shared in his memory, and the resurrection faith that he was raised "on the third day," were first felt by these grieving women.[17] Their proclamation that Jesus is risen was not a triumphalist declaration that his death was undone by divine fiat and their grief blessedly ended. To say "He is risen" was to name that grief itself, to describe the acts of care performed in his name by a community haunted by his absence, to speak a lack filled with longing.

In the faith of these women—these first Christians—there seems to have been no opposition between mourning and resurrection. They are the same. The theologian Angela Standhartinger, building off Cor-

17. See especially Kathleen E. Corley, *Maranatha: Women's Funerary Rituals and Christian Origins* (Minneapolis: Fortress Press, 2010), 89–132.

ley's work, writes that Hellenistic women's mourning songs and funerary meals were themselves experiences of the resurrection of the dead. "Through their mouths and bodies," Standhartinger writes, "the lamenters raise[d] the dead by allowing them to speak symbolic words through their voices and perform symbolic acts through their bodies."[18] The absence of the dead was both irrevocable and somehow more than absence, as the dead beloved's voice was heard again in the keening of the bereaved, their hunger encountered again in the hunger of the grieving, their absence made viscerally present in the very work of mourning.

Loss is not overcome in such a theology of resurrection; rather the lost love is present in and as the loss itself. While the earliest version of the Gospel of Mark ends with a startling scene of absence, fear, and confusion, the very fact that such a Gospel exists shows the women did not remain scattered and silent forever. Eventually they gathered to solace one another in their sorrow, to weep together, to sing of the one they had lost, to share bread and wine. And though remaining

18. Angela Standhartinger, "Bringing Back to Life: Laments and the Origin of the So-Called Words of Institution," in *Coming Back to Life: The Permeability of Past and Present, Mortality and Immortality, Death and Life in the Ancient Mediterranean*, ed. Frederick S. Tappenden and Carly Daniel-Hughes (Montreal: McGill University Library, 2017), 71–102, 90.

disconsoled, they felt him beside them in their sorrow, hearing his comfort in the comfort they spoke.[19]

Though Standhartinger describes ancient Palestinian mourning rituals as raising the dead through "symbolic" acts, the Christology of the Gospels describes a more than symbolic resurrection. One of the memories that Jesus's friends told and retold after his death was their last meal together. At that meal, John tells us, Jesus gave his friends a new commandment: "As I have loved you, so should you love one another." Adrienne von Speyr, in a commentary she wrote on the book of John, dwells at length on this verse. Jesus tells his friends to love each other, she points out, "at the moment which he promises that they will seek but not find him." He promises his friends that he will be gone and they will grieve, and he commands them to love each other in their grief. And while he reminds them again and again of his coming absence, he also promises they will yet see him. This paradox—they will lose him, but in losing him they will have him—is possible because Jesus is himself love.[20]

The sorrowing love the disciples will feel in his absence, a love they will enact by comforting each

19. I take this idea of a comfort that remains "disconsoling" from Timothy P. Jackson, *Love Disconsoled: Meditations on Christian Charity* (Cambridge: Cambridge University Press, 1999).

20. Von Speyr, *The Farewell Discourses*, 66.

other in their shared grief, is his own self. "He creates for them a substitute, as it were," von Speyr writes. "But it is more than a substitute, because this commandment is his gift, because he lives in this gift." He lives in the gift of their sad longing that will not be satisfied because he himself is God's infinite longing. The longing that will draw his friends into the place where he is not, where they will not find him but will find each other, the longing that will draw the love of their sorrowing hearts ever outward—this is him. They will not find him where they expect to find him. The tomb is empty. Instead they must *realize* (in both senses: they must recognize and they must make real) the God who is love by living out that love with and for others. All others. "He is in each one whom he loves," von Speyr writes, "and he loves everyone." [21]

The account of resurrection I'm tracing here is no "demythologization." My claim is not that Jesus didn't *really* rise from the dead, so we can interpret the community of his followers or the faith he left behind as his risen body. Such demythologization, warns theologian Matthew Ichihashi Potts, only repeats the "happy ending" it pretends to overcome. Celebrating the gathered community as the restored presence of Jesus, a demythologized reading of his resurrection refuses the

---

21. Von Speyr, *The Farewell Discourses*, 66.

void of his absence, rushing to fill the empty tomb with a too-easy story of recuperation.[22]

The theology of resurrection we can learn from those grieving women in ancient Palestine, however, is one of void and want. In keeping open the painful wound of loss, in remaining disconsoled, we remain faithful to Jesus's resurrection. Recall Hadewijch's theology of *Minne*: the love that is God is a longing that will not be satisfied. If Jesus is this longing incarnate, then both a crude reading of resurrection as restoration and a sober demythologization would be refusals of his resurrection, in that both proffer the end of longing. What those first Christian women understood, and what we in the twilight of the Christian West need to relearn, is the mystery that the resurrected Jesus is present in and as the want of him. He is encountered as risen in the restless searching that fails ever to find him, because to long for him is already to have him, because he is this very desire.

Those first women who gathered in graveyards to weep together and feed each other knew well that resurrection is more haunting and grief than permanence and reward. For them, to say Jesus is risen was not to say that their loss had been undone but to proclaim that

22. Matthew Ichihashi Potts, *Forgiveness: An Alternative Account* (New Haven, CT: Yale University Press, 2022), 211–12.

love is stronger than death, that the love that he was remains yet and might be known again in loving others. The theology of mourning this book has been laying out—that God is present in and as God's absence, that transience and lack are not temporary embarrassments from which God will save us but the groundless ground of God's love, that we find Jesus not by preserving our present way of life but by walking alongside others into an unknown future—therefore proclaims Christ resurrected.

❧

For twentieth-century antifascists like Georges Bataille and Simone Weil, the creedal claim that Jesus rose again on the third day is a political landmine lodged in the heart of the Christian tradition. What began as a grieving community gathered to mourn the loss of one they had loved, a mourning faith that the Gospel writers turned to as they looked for ways to resist the brutality of empire, became in the end the legitimating theology of empire itself—a self-betrayal that Bataille and Weil blamed on the theology of resurrection. They believed the claim Jesus rose from the dead conditioned those born in historically Christian societies to view transience and loss as threats that could be eliminated with sufficient force. And they saw fascism as exploiting this expectation, as the fascist leader promised to purify the nation and secure it everlastingly through limitless violence against the unworthy.

If there was any hope for an antifascist form of Christianity, thought Bataille and Weil, it must be a Christianity without resurrection—thus, as both admit, not really Christianity at all. Bataille spent the 1930s and '40s engaged in increasingly outrageous subversions of Christian thought and practice he (semi-) ironically called "hyperchristianity," while Simone Weil refused to be baptized and instead cobbled together her own idiosyncratic devotion to the cross out of various religious traditions.[23] For them, only by jettisoning resurrection and thereby undoing itself could Christianity hope to resist the fascist politics to which it had given rise.

Bataille and Weil rightly show the dangers of a triumphalist reading of resurrection. But they were too quick to believe that a tragic and mournful reading of Jesus's death necessarily puts one beyond the bounds of resurrection faith. In fact, such a sorrowful reading of resurrection is perhaps more faithful to the earliest roots of the Christian tradition—those grieving women

23. Georges Bataille, *On Nietzsche*, trans. Bruce Boone (New York: Paragon House, 1994).

in ancient Palestine feeding one another and singing songs of lamentation—than any triumphalist one.

As the Gospel writers knew, those ancient mourners show us a way of imagining resurrection beyond power and permanence. In the spirit of Bataille and Weil, then, we might learn to resist the revolt against mourning gripping what remains of the Christian West by learning from those first Christian women a genuinely tragic theology of resurrection. What might it look like to take them as our guides for becoming what Rowan Williams calls communities of resurrection? As Williams says elsewhere, to seek God "is not to seek for timeless vision, for the true and the eternal, as a kind of *place* to escape from the vicissitudes of the material world." Instead Christian faith "must enact its yearning through the corporate life of persons in the world."[24] What might our corporate life look like if we imagined resurrection not as the end of our yearning for one who is not here, but its beginning?

Encounters with other persons in the world are necessarily unpredictable and fleeting and transformative; it is only in inviting a wanderer to dinner, in listening to a graveyard laborer, in sitting down to dinner with a stranger on a beach that the disciples felt the near-

24. Rowan Williams, "Language, Reality and Desire in Augustine's *De Doctrina*," *Journal of Literature and Theology* 3, no. 2 (July 1989): 138–50 (145).

ness of the one whom they had lost. If the movement of withdrawal that is the love of God is a love that effaces itself and makes room so that another can arise into the now-empty space, then we meet that love on the far side of the cross when we live it out, when we make that love real in our encounters with others. To be faithful to the resurrection, then, we must open ourselves to transience and loss, to transformation and change, to the passing of what we have known and the coming of the strange.

CHAPTER 6

Michel de Certeau
Mourning Christianity

"There is an outstanding 1973 book," Viktor Orbán digressed during the 2022 speech discussed in chapter 4. He went on to enthusiastically recommend the book to anyone wanting to understand "the spiritual developments underlying the West's inability to defend itself" against "population replacement or inundation."[1] The book in question is a novel by the French travel writer Jean Raspail, titled *The Camp of the Saints*. Raspail's novel has been hailed by leading voices on the global right as shrewdly predicting the crises currently afflicting the West. Its admirers include pundits like Steve Bannon, government officials like Stephen Miller, political leaders like Marine Le Pen, and members of Italian prime minister Giorgia Meloni's Brothers of Italy party.

1. Orbán, "Speech by Prime Minister Viktor Orbán at the 31st Bálványos Summer Free University and Student Camp."

When *The Camp of the Saints* is described in liberal media, it's often called a "racist novel." That's a polite euphemism for what is in fact a fascist fever dream, a hallucinatory fantasy of racial apocalypse in which the white race is exterminated by a rapidly breeding swarm of subhuman nonwhite migrants. The plot, such as it is, involves a ragtag fleet of refugees from nonwhite countries setting sail for Europe, the fleet growing as more and more people join in their makeshift boats, until eventually they're welcomed to Europe by naïve liberals and quickly set about destroying everything.

When the book isn't describing people of color as "vermin," "monsters," "dogs," or "mildew," it's subjecting the reader to pornographic scenes of the mass of teeming flesh crashing on Europe's shores.[2] In one of the many passages in which the novel drops all pretense of storytelling to directly harangue the reader, whites are described as "the chosen people" and are told if they are to merit God's favor and protection then "the time [has] come to steel their souls once more, cast out all pity in a single night," and kill as many immigrants as possible.[3]

It's impossible to overstate how artless and blood-thirsty the book is—less a novel than a manifesto, a

2. Jean Raspail, *The Camp of the Saints*, trans. Norman Shapiro (New York: Scribner, 1975), 107, 23, 54, 296.

3. Raspail, *The Camp of the Saints*, 110.

genocidal howl for white people to unite and exterminate those "human ants" beyond the walls of Christendom before it's too late.[4]

When *The Camp of the Saints* is described by the
politicians and pundits of the global right, however, it's
hailed as a prophetic work of art. In *National Review*,
Mackubin Thomas Owens, former professor and dean at
the U.S. Naval War College, wrote that the novel "eerily
prefigures" how "Christendom" is set to be "swamped"
by immigrants.[5] In *The European Conservative*, the
former U.S. State Department official Alberto Fernandez described the novel as "eerily prescient."[6] And
from his column at the *American Conservative* that ran
from 2015 to 2020, Rod Dreher became something of
an evangelist for Raspail's novel, publishing essays like
"America's *Camp of the Saints* Problem," "America's
Camp of the Saints," "It Really Is *Camp of the Saints*,"
"Francis & the Camp of the Saints," "What I Learned
from *The Camp of the Saints*," and on and on. The radical right considers Raspail a prophetic figure, able to

4. Raspail, *The Camp of the Saints*, 308.

5. Mackubin Thomas Owens, "What an Off-Putting French
Novel Can Tell Us about Immigration," *National Review* (blog),
June 13, 2014, https://www.nationalreview.com/2014/06/camp-
saints-2014-style-mackubin-thomas-owens/.

6. Alberto M. Fernandez, "Go North," *The European Conservative*, November 16, 2024, https://europeanconservative.
com/articles/reviews/go-north/.

peer from the 1970s into our present—eerily, always "eerily"—and see the death of the Christian West at the hands of desperate and hungry outsiders. (Those who praise its eerie prescience leave unasked the question of just how "prophetic" is its proposed solution of total race war or its gleeful depictions of plucky white heroes hunting migrants for sport.)

Raspail is a prophet, according to his devotees, because his position as a French Catholic at the turn of the 1970s gave him special insight into just how precarious the Christian West is. For those on the right, the turn of the 1970s was a kind of dress rehearsal for the present. The twilight of the Christian West seemed at hand, and today dusk really is falling, so we can read those who lived through its apparent end back then to learn how to live through its real end today.

It was not unreasonable for a French Catholic in the early 1970s to feel that he was living through the collapse of a familiar Western Christian culture. Then as now, the world really was rapidly changing. In 1958, the French constitution formally declared France a secular republic. In the early 1960s, the Second Vatican Council announced a new policy of *aggiornamento*, according to which the church would adapt to the world rather than demand the world adapt to the church. In the wake of World War II, the French colonial empire contracted rapidly: in 1954, France lost control over Indochina; in

1956, Morocco; in 1960, West Africa; in 1962, Algeria. Those formerly subordinated in the colonies began migrating in huge numbers to the country that had for so long enriched itself on their backs and that, after the war, was desperate for laborers.[7] As the church and the empire appeared to dissolve, so too did the family. Women gained the right to work independently and to hold their own bank accounts in 1965; birth control was legalized in 1967; and in 1970 France officially discarded the old rule of *puissance paternelle*, according to which fathers held absolute parental authority over their children. Everything came to a head in May 1968, when the world's revolutionary and decolonial shocks came home. France was roiled by protests and general strikes when far-left students joined with trade unions to bring the French economy to a halt. President Charles de Gaulle, fearing total collapse, fled to Germany.

Wherever Raspail would have looked, he would have seen dusk descending on a familiar world order and a strange, unruly, unfamiliar day dawning. He turned his pessimism into fable, one he hoped would galvanize what remained of the Christian West to defend itself before it went under.

7. Félix F. Germain, *Decolonizing the Republic: African and Caribbean Migrants in Postwar Paris, 1946–1974* (East Lansing: Michigan State University Press, 2016).

Fifty years later, as our world undergoes its own imperial decline, secularization, accelerating migration, frequent mass protests, and rapid rearrangement of gender and the family, Raspail's novel has been picked from the bargain bin and dusted off and declared a prophecy. In the right's reading, *The Camp of the Saints* recorded the first whisper of the Christian West's death rattle, a whisper now heaving toward its final end.

As in the 1970s, the global right today isn't wrong to feel a familiar arrangement of religion, gender, ethnicity, culture, and power—the Christian West—is passing away while shifting and unfamiliar arrangements take its place. Where they go wrong is their understanding of what the end of this arrangement means. They see it as a catastrophe, a defeat imposed by barbarous enemies and smirking traitors, some awful humiliation that must be fought off at all costs.

There are better guides through the twilight of the Christian West than Raspail and his bloodthirsty revolt against mourning. There were others who lived through the same cultural shocks of the 1960s and '70s and who shared the same sense that a familiar world was giving way to something new and strange, yet who unlike Raspail had the strength to mourn. These others found in the work of grieving their loss and moving forward into an unknown future a new and deeper faith. In this last chapter, we will look to the turn of the 1970s, that moment when it seemed dusk was falling for the Christian West, and learn from these other voices how to better live through its twilight.

෴

The turn of the 1970s gave rise to a wild profusion of theological reflection on the end of Western Christian hegemony. Those were the years of liberation theology, of Gustavo Gutierrez's *A Theology of Liberation* and James Cone's *Black Theology and Black Power*. They were also years of avowedly feminist theology, like Mary Daly's *Beyond God the Father* and Rosemary Ruether's *The Church Against Itself*, when the "Philadelphia Eleven" became the first women ordained as priests in the Episcopal Church. These years saw the birth pangs of queer-affirming churches, with the founding of the Metropolitan Community Church outside Los Angeles and the first same-sex marriage celebrated in the United States occurring at Minneapolis's Hennepin Avenue United Methodist Church. As the Christian West grew quieter, voices that had been historically silenced made themselves heard.

Instead of that crescendo, however, this chapter will listen a while longer to the fading voices. The reason why the right finds Raspail so prophetic is because he approached the death of the Christian West as someone with something to lose. He felt he had a place in the Christian France of old, and the rapid disappearance of that familiar culture left him feeling unmoored. For him, its passing away was a painful loss. Those today who live on the underside of the Christian West might experience its death not as loss but as gain, turning to liberation or feminist or queer theologies from the 1970s as guides for how to navigate the space opened by a contracting hegemony. But I want to sit with that feeling of loss that so wounded Raspail and continues to wound his acolytes today.

I want to sit with it because I share it. As a straight, white, Christian man, someone for whom that peculiar arrangement I've been calling the Christian West has made a place, the loss of that place—however ambivalent I may feel about it—is a genuine loss. The philosopher Judith Butler has acknowledged that people like myself have much to lose as Western Christian hegemony fades. They counsel us to "start that process of mourning," to refuse "destructive rage" and instead carry out the difficult work of "productive grief."[8] Instead of joining Raspail in his destructive rage, as the pundits and the leaders of the global right urge us to do, we must instead learn from others in the 1970s who had

8. Butler, *Who's Afraid of Gender?*, 237.

a great deal to lose yet who had the strength to productively grieve their loss.

༜

There are a few voices from the turn of the 1970s who experienced the seemingly immanent end of the Christian West as a genuine loss yet who attempted to construct theologies of mourning. Writing from Cambridge in 1968, the Scottish theologian Donald MacKinnon lamented how, for too many, "Christian life is identified with the continuance of a particular cultural complex, of which Christian faith is judged a constituent part."[9] When that happens, any change in that cultural complex is experienced as an existential threat to faith itself. (We see this today. Take, for example, Patrick Deneen, who frets that the mere presence of "black studies, women's studies, gay studies, etc." departments on college campuses is the first step toward the "effective elimination" of straight, white, Christian men.)[10] Instead of this jumpy panic, MacKinnon urged his readers to "receive as a profound liberation the disintegration of what we still inaccurately call our 'Christian culture.'"[11] The falling silent of Western Christian speech, for MacKinnon,

9. MacKinnon, *Borderlands of Theology*, 36.
10. Deneen, *Regime Change*, 168–69.
11. MacKinnon, *Borderlands of Theology*, 36.

was a kind of mystical unsaying preceding new and unexpected reverberations of the Word.

Similarly, in the United States, the Catholic writer Garry Wills shared with his conservative friends the feeling that the Second Vatican Council was hastening the death of the Catholic Church in Europe and North America. But he insisted this death could be met with something other than reactionary pseudo-traditionalism. The loudest defenders of Christian tradition, he noted acidly, treated the church not as a place of living faith but a fetish object warding off the fear of death, nothing more than "some obscure pledge of the relevance of older things."[12] A truly living faith, Wills wrote, is one that consents to die, because life is at every moment loss and transformation. The death of any particular form of Christian life reveals that Christian life was never just *this*, that God's Word always exceeds whatever meager words we use to capture it. "Christianity did not leave the Temple once for all," Wills wrote; "it must go out constantly from new temples."[13] He urged his fellow white American Catholics to approach the seeming death of their own particular forms of Christianity with just this kind of mournful trust that, though they grieve, the Word of God speaks yet.

12. Garry Wills, *Bare Ruined Choirs: Doubt, Prophecy, and Radical Religion* (New York: Delta, 1972), 1.
13. Wills, *Bare Ruined Choirs,* 212.

But the fullest articulation of a theology of mourning from this period comes from a French Jesuit theologian named Michel de Certeau. Certeau's and Raspail's lives fascinatingly refract into each other. Both were born in France in 1925, spending their childhoods and adolescences in conditions of war and occupation. Yet they experienced the war quite differently: Certeau spent the war years in the Alps passing messages between Resistance groups, while Raspail was in occupied Paris being mentored by the author of a pamphlet titled *Jewish Peril*.[14]

After the war, Certeau entered the Jesuit order, hoping to be sent to China so he could explore the world. But the Communists were expelling the Jesuits and, obedient to his order, Certeau remained in France. Meanwhile, Raspail was living Certeau's dream, leading an expedition deep into rural Peru and an odyssey by car from the tip of South America to the top of Alaska.

As the 1960s passed into the 1970s, both men experienced their historical moment as a disorienting shock, the twilight of a familiar Christian world. Certeau

14. Natalie Zemon Davis, "The Quest of Michel de Certeau," *New York Review of Books*, May 15, 2008; Marc Weitzmann, "A Visit with Jean Raspail, Creator of 'The Great Replacement' Theory," *Tablet Magazine*, March 28, 2017, https://www.tablet mag.com/sections/news/articles/steve-bannon-jean-raspail.

described "feeling the Christian ground on which I thought I was walking disappear, seeing the messengers of an ending, long time under way, approach."[15] But where Raspail's grief curdled into maudlin travelogues and fascistic novels, Certeau's grief led him to write some of the most profound and moving theological essays ever written.

In these essays, Certeau lays out a vision of Christianity in which the Christian life is none other than an endless work of "impossible mourning."[16] It's fitting, then, to end this book's theology of mourning with Certeau. He lights a path through the twilight of the Christian West, down which we might discover in the depths of our mourning new ways of being Christian.

ॐ

"Christianity was founded upon *the loss of a body*," Michel de Certeau writes. "A founding disappearance indeed." Each of the four Gospels' resurrection stories tell this loss differently: the terror and silence in Mark, the abrupt sending away of the women in Matthew, the mysterious appearances and disappearances in Luke,

15. Michel de Certeau, "The Weakness of Believing. From the Body to Writing, a Christian Transit," in *The Certeau Reader*, ed. Graham Ward; trans. Saskia Brown (Malden, MA: Blackwell, 2000), 230.

16. Certeau, *The Mystic Fable*, 1:81.

Jesus's "Don't touch me" in John. Each story revolves around a central moment in which those who come to the tomb to find Jesus instead find—nothing. Even the Gospels that narrate resurrection appearances end with the ascension, with Jesus gone.

The Synoptic Gospels plainly state the loss with the angel's words: "He is not here; he has gone to Galilee." For Certeau, these words inaugurate Christianity as a ceaseless wandering and searching, a forever-unsatisfied yearning for one who is always elsewhere. The tomb is empty. He is not here.

If living as a Christian means answering Jesus's call to follow him, then, as Certeau suggests, we must reckon with the fact that this call "comes from a voice which has been effaced, forever irrecuperable, vanished into the changes which echo it back, drowned in the throng of its respondents."[17]

On one hand, this is a straightforward description of the Christian condition. The Gospels, after all, are not one single text but four contradictory and confused versions of the same life story. Did Jesus deliver the beatitudes on a mount or a plain? Was he killed before or after Passover? Skeptical readers have for generations latched onto these differences as proof of some mistak-

17. Certeau, "The Weakness of Believing," 227.

enness in the Gospels. But, for Certeau, the contradictions are the point.

Jesus didn't set down some final account of who he is and what his life and death mean, penned in his own hand and sealed with his signature. Instead he handed his story over to others. In this founding dispossession, Certeau sees the heart of all Christology: Jesus is the one who hands himself over.

This is the christological truth that the four Gospels reveal, and they reveal it precisely because they are confused and contradictory, and because their status as "canonical" gestures to their own noncanonical outside, to a wild array of other responses to the life and death of Jesus popping up and fading away beyond the confines of the official church. *Who Jesus is* is the one who gives up control over himself and his story to others who will respond in unpredictable ways.

Think of Weil's claim that creation, incarnation, and passion are one single movement of divine withdrawal, or Bonhoeffer's insistence that when we speak of Jesus's divinity we should speak only of his birth in a manger and his death on a cross. In the incarnation, his helpless infant body is taken into Mary's hands. In the Eucharist, he presses his body as bread into the hands of his friends, even the friend who has betrayed him. During his arrest and crucifixion, he is seized by the violent hands of the state. And in the stories that arose in his wake, he surrenders any authorial control and lets others say who he is and what his story means. "The Christian language begins with the disappearance of its 'author,'" Certeau writes.[18]

This founding disappearance has its narrative center in the stories of the empty tomb. Jesus withdraws, leaving a void where once he was, and in that emptiness proliferate texts and communities that will tell of the transformations he awakened in them. Whatever access we have to Jesus is not direct and unmediated, as if he were somewhere we could go to see with our own eyes or hear with our own ears or touch with our own fingers. Instead he is always mediated to us by others. This is the point Bonhoeffer made in his dissertation: We hear stories of Jesus told to us by others; we see the changes worked in others' lives by their responding to his call; we touch others whose lives have been touched by others, an endless chain of responses to responses to responses. This is why Certeau, a founding member of the École freudienne de Paris, views Christian faith as an endless work of mourning in Freud's sense of the term: forever attached to a lost love, we are forever drawn outside of ourselves and toward the transforming presence of others.

18. Certeau, "How Is Christianity Thinkable Today?," 145.

Certeau also makes clear the political demands of this theology of mourning. "Since Jesus," he writes, "an internal law links his death to the necessity of making room for others. It expresses an essential covenant of Christianity with the unforeseeable or unknown spaces which God opens everywhere and in other ways."[19] The *necessity* of making room for others. As in Weil's creation theology, God is for Certeau the one who gives up space so that others can fill it. That is the sum and substance of Christ's divinity, and the Christian life is the work of living out this self-effacing love in the world.

To say that Jesus is divine is to say that he *just is* this love that makes room for others and opens unknown spaces. Where Weil describes this divine withdrawal as the origin of the world, Certeau describes it as the origin of the church. Recall Henri de Lubac's statement that eucharistic theology is a meditation on the "three bodies of Christ." "The body of Christ" refers at once to the historical body of Jesus, the consecrated bread of the Eucharist, and the community that shares the bread. For Certeau, it is because the tomb is empty and Jesus's historical body is absent that the bread and the community can arise as his body. It is because his voice has faded away into silence that others can speak of what he made possible.

19. Certeau, "How Is Christianity Thinkable Today?," 150.

Like the women at the tomb, we are driven by Jesus's absence to search for him. And we search for him not by sealing up the tomb and declaring that here and nowhere else is all goodness and holiness. That would be what theologian Louis-Marie Chauvet calls the "necrotic temptation" haunting Christianity: the temptation to hold fast to a body that we must instead learn to let go.[20]

Renouncing the necrotic temptation means "going to Galilee," looking ever elsewhere, stepping out from the familiar hollow of the tomb and into an unknown future filled with unknown others. In Certeau's words, Christians have in every age "continued to wonder, 'Where art thou?' And from century to century they ask history as it passes: 'Where have you put him?'"[21] The proper Christian posture toward the non-Christian world is not what he calls "missionary totalism," in which we imagine ourselves to have something others don't and work to make them more like us.[22] Instead, we're called to a perpetual wondering and wandering, humbly approaching others as perhaps having what we lack and long for.

As I noted earlier, Certeau shares with Raspail a sense that the death of a recognizable Christian West

20. Chauvet, *Symbol and Sacrament*, 174.
21. Certeau, *The Mystic Fable,* 1:82.
22. Certeau, "How Is Christianity Thinkable Today?," 150.

is a genuine loss. Certeau is no pollyannaish liberal blithely tossing away the old and embracing the new simply because it's new. He too grieves the loss of a familiar Christian culture. Where the two differ is in their sense of what this loss means.

For Raspail, the loss is a kind of castration. *The Camp of the Saints*'s pornographic terror is a case study in castration anxiety. And today's right, sharing Raspail's obsession with white people being "outbred," takes him as their guide to warding off castration through racialized violence.

Certeau, on the other hand, maintains that the loss of a recognizable form of Christian life is a real loss, while at the same time insisting that such loss is the meaning of Christian life in the first place. Christianity was always "destined to lose itself in history."[23] The death of a particular form of Christianity is not a wound inflicted on us by some blameworthy other who can and must be stopped with force, but is instead the very movement of God's self-effacing grace.

Jesus, writes Certeau, "had to be 'here' in order that it might be possible for him to be 'not here' but 'elsewhere'; he had to be present so that his disappearance might become the sign of a different future." If the church is to truly be the body of Christ, then it

23. Certeau, "The Weakness of Believing," 229.

too must follow this movement of disappearance and departure. To be "not here" anymore is for Certeau the raison d'être of any Christian community. Christianity is a "movement," he writes, and so any concrete form of Christian community is not a thing to shore up and defend but a place from which to move elsewhere. "A particular place—our particular place—is required if there is to be a departure."[24]

"Departing without return," mourning the loss of a place we cannot get back while moving into a place we cannot predict, is the true shape of Christian life.[25] If we are to follow the one who is not here but always elsewhere, then we too must consent to lose our "here" and disappear into an uncertain and unknown future.

This kind of mourning Christianity, put into practice, looks not like defending or spreading "our way of life" but surrendering control over it, allowing the communities in which we live and work and worship to be transformed by new relationships of solidarity and love with others. To bring things back to our discussion of Weil's creation theology, it looks a lot like what gets demonized these days as "replacement." It looks like remaining ever open to, in Certeau's words, "the grace of being altered by what comes."[26]

24. Certeau, "How Is Christianity Thinkable Today?," 151.
25. Certeau, "The Weakness of Believing," 228.
26. Certeau, "The Weakness of Believing," 229.

⌇

At the end of *The Camp of the Saints*, the "People's Assembly of the Paris Multiracial Commune" is inaugurated in a grand ceremony during which the archbishop of Paris publicly embraces the grand mufti of Jerusalem and "[makes] him a present of some thirty churches, to be turned into mosques."[27] (In case the racism is somehow too subtle, the next paragraph describes white women married to nonwhite men as "symbols of the death of the race.") Indeed, the sight of mosques in Western cities remains a profound psychic trauma for the right. Recall the controversy over the so-called Ground Zero Mosque in New York City (really a community center two blocks away), or the 2009 referendum in Switzerland banning minarets, the tall towers attached to mosques.[28] Proposals proliferate across the West to demolish mosques, ban their construction, or otherwise force Muslim worship underground, put forward by far-right leaders like the Netherland's Geert

27. Raspail, *The Camp of the Saints*, 293.
28. Anne Barnard, "Painful Memory for Muslims: Outrage over a Proposed Islamic Center in Manhattan," *New York Times*, September 11, 2021, https://www.nytimes.com/2021/09/11/ny region/muslim-islamic-center-9-11.html; "Swiss Voters Back Ban on Minarets," BBC News, November 29, 2009, http://news. bbc.co.uk/2/hi/8385069.stm.

Wilders, Sweden's Jimmy Åkesson, and Italy's Giorgia Meloni—to say nothing of Donald Trump's infamous attempt in 2017 to ban Muslims from entering the United States altogether.[29] A mosque is not simply a sign that Muslims live here but is a material space in which Muslims visibly participate in public life. People worship there, and they also organize; they provide and receive care such as food and housing; they issue calls to prayer that can be heard by those who are not Muslim. For Raspail and his acolytes, the mosque is not just a symptom but a cause of the "replacement" of the Christian West. That a mosque could stand where a church once stood is for the radical right the ultimate horror.

But for Certeau, when a historically Christian community cedes space to a material site of cultural difference like a mosque, that Christian community is more fully following Jesus's call to follow him. To be

29. "Memorie van Toelichting—Voorstel van Wet van de Leden Wilders En De Graaf Betreffende Het Verbod van Bepaalde Islamitische Uitingen," *Parlementaire Monitor*, September 22, 2018, https://www.parlementairemonitor.nl/9353 000/1/j9vvij5epmj1ey0/vkrzacfdiyzk; "Swedish PM Rebukes Far-Right Leader Who Said Mosques Should Be Flattened," Politico.eu, November 27, 2023, https://www.politico.eu/article/ swedish-pm-ulf-kristersson-slams-far-right-party-leader-for-suggesting-mosques-should-be-demolished/; O'Reilly, "Meloni Building Regulations Target Mosques," The European Conservative, June 13, 2023, https://europeanconservative.com/ articles/news/meloni-building-regulations-target-mosques/.

Christian is (to take a phrase from Bonhoeffer) to be "formed to the form of Christ," and the form of Christ is one who lives wholly for others, disappearing and giving rise to endless differentiation.[30] Conversely, to ban mosques in the name of preserving Christianity is to refuse the grace of being altered by what comes, paradoxically destroying what one is trying to preserve. Such efforts reduce Christianity to, in Certeau's words, "a (perhaps beautiful) museum, a (perhaps glorious) cemetery."[31] By a corresponding paradox, it's only by consenting to lose Christianity that we keep open the possibility of responding to Jesus's call to follow him. As he himself said, "Those who want to save their life will lose it, and those who lose their life for my sake will find it" (Matthew 16:25).

॰ॐ

The last light of the Christian West is fading. Whether we will it or not, whether we approach this age of the Greatest Migration with welcome and solidarity or with fear and violence, our world is changing. We can, like Raspail, revolt against mourning, clinging with all

30. Dietrich Bonhoeffer, *Ethics*, ed. Clifford J. Green; trans. Reinhard Krauss, Charles C. West, and Douglas W. Stott; Dietrich Bonhoeffer Works 6 (Minneapolis: Fortress Press, 2009), 92.

31. Certeau, "How Is Christianity Thinkable Today?," 155.

the greater intensity to what is left, lashing out at anyone outside our ever-dwindling circle of "us."

But Certeau shows a different way through the twilight. In the last years of his life, he traced the outline of a mourning Christianity, a Christianity that truly lives because it consents at each moment to lose itself. "Always on the move," he wrote of such a Christianity,

> in practices of reading which are increasingly heterogeneous and distant from any ecclesial orthodoxy, [Jesus's call] announced the disappearance of the site. Having passed that way, it left, as at Bethel, only the trace of stones erected into stelae and consecrated with oil—with our gratitude—before departing without return.[32]

For those of us who feel unmoored in these last days of the Christian West, we can find here a way to mourn, and so a way to live. Consecrate these scattered stones and depart. We will not return.

As our mourning pulls us elsewhere, we might find grace in being altered by what comes, in listening with silent attention to the incomprehensible words of the strangest stranger as perhaps an echo of the ever silent yet ever speaking Word.

32. Certeau, "The Weakness of Believing," 228.

Epilogue

In the story "The Last Witness" by the Argentine writer Jorge Luis Borges, an old man lies in the shadow of a new church, "meekly seeking death like someone seeking sleep." It is sometime in the eleventh century, and the dying man is the last person left with any memory of England's pre-Christian religions. "The man, while still a boy, had seen the faces of Woden, had seen holy dread and exultation, had seen the rude wooden idol weighed down with Roman coins and heavy vestments, seen the sacrifice of horses, dogs, and prisoners."

And now he is dying. "Before dawn he would be dead and with him would die, never to return, the last firsthand images of the pagan rites. The world would be poorer when this Saxon was no more." In the end, Borges's narrator reflects, we are all the old dying Saxon. "Something, or an infinite number of things, die in each death . . . What will die with me when I die? What pathetic or frail form will the world lose?"[1]

1. Jorge Luis Borges, *Labyrinths*, ed. Donald A. Yates and James E. Irby (New York: New Directions, 1964), 243.

I thought of Borges's story on Good Friday one year, as I attended mass at the Society of St. John the Evangelist, an Episcopal monastery on the bank of the Charles River. The service ended quietly, anticlimactically, with soft singing fading into silence and everyone trickling out alone. Lingering for a bit afterward, I sat alongside a few others in front of the tabernacle. During the Maundy Thursday service the night before, the consecrated bread that for the rest of the year is stored in the tabernacle was moved away. The usual way of understanding this ritual is that the consecrated bread is the real presence of Jesus, and on Good Friday, the day commemorating his death, the bread is likewise taken away from us, repeating what Certeau called our founding disappearance.

But that evening—and I confess I'm not one for "religious experiences"—I felt something different. The feeling of loss and absence was foremost, but underneath it was another feeling, something like presence. The bread had been taken away, and in its place was an emptiness. Yet I recalled Hadewijch, Angela, Bonhoeffer, Weil, von Speyr, and Certeau, for whom emptiness, withdrawal, and being taken away are the very movement of God's self-effacing love. In creation, God effaces Godself to make the world; in the incarnation, God gives up what we imagine as divinity to live as a squalling infant; in the passion, Jesus renounces self-preservation and retaliation to lay down his life in love; in the Eucharist, he empties himself into the fragile works of bread and wine; in the resurrection, he leaves the tomb empty; in the ascension, he withdraws from his friends and leaves behind a bewildered, loving community. Always the same movement of withdrawal, as Weil said. Recalling her words, I felt the emptiness of the tabernacle on that Good Friday evening, the nothing at all inside it and the scattered few around it, as itself the presence of God's love, the strange presence of a love lived as effacement and lack. Void is not only void. It is also the space where the absent presence of love comes alive.

I thought of Borges's story as I walked home that night because the scattered few around the empty tabernacle that year was a little more scattered and a little fewer than the year before, and more so than the year before that, and before that. Someday, I thought—not just yet, but the day is coming—someone will die, and with them will die, never to return, the last firsthand images of the Christian West. Christianity is destined, as Certeau wrote, to lose itself in history. Whatever particular form of Christian life in which we find ourselves, that form is a finite thing, something that arose in time and will, in time, disappear. One day every church in Europe and North America, and then one day long afterward every church in the world, will be as empty as that Good Friday tabernacle.

How will we respond to the inevitability of our disappearance? Will we revolt against mourning, gathering what force we can muster to preserve these pathetic frail forms from being replaced by others? Or will we learn to see our withdrawal, our disappearance into history, as our way of being pulled along into the withdrawing current of God's love? Will we see the empty space we leave behind as something more than void, as a space in which new loves can arise? Will we have the strength to mourn?

Dietrich Bonhoeffer imagined a Christianity beyond self-preservation, one that could view the falling silent of its great and ancient words as a death on the other side of which might arise unfamiliar and unexpected life. This life after the death of the Christian West could be found, he wrote, in silent prayer and acts of loving solidarity. "The words we used before must lose their power, be silenced, and we can be Christians today only in two ways, through prayer and in doing justice among human beings."[2]

Twilight, after all, is not only the gathering dark of dusk. It's also the first light of a new and wholly different dawn.

2. Bonhoeffer, *Letters and Papers from Prison*, 389.

ACKNOWLEDGMENTS

There is not room to name all of the colleagues, friends, and loved ones who have shaped my thinking and so shaped this book, so I will limit myself to just a few. Michael Putnam, my most loyal reader, read every word of this book in at least five different versions; for nearly ten years now almost every idea I've had has been honed in our conversations, and this book simply would not exist without him. Evan Goldstein read one of the earliest drafts of a chapter and pulled me back from a dead-end road. Kelsey Hanson Woodruff swapped drafts with me, and I can't wait for her own book to appear. Sally Hansen talked with me for hours on the phone as I worked through my ideas. Br. Keith Nelson spurred me to consider in more depth how the ideas in this book might be lived. Matt Potts has been my most influential teacher of theology, as well as a true friend; he read drafts of chapters, gave much-needed encouragement, and helped me see a structure for the book. Many of the texts discussed in this book I first read in classes with him. Lindsay Lerman was the first person to read

195

the complete manuscript, and our conversations always reminded me why, despite it all, I do in fact love writing. Jess Mesman lit the first spark of this being a book project through her enthusiasm and support for my writing in *The Christian Century* and by putting me in touch with Orbis Books. Particular thanks are due my editor at Orbis, Lil Copan, for bringing clarity to what was at times a confusing mess even to me. My parents, Sally and Stephen, and my brother, Luke, have been as always bedrocks of love and support. Nikki, Tim, Emily, and Jill, in teaching me so much about friendship, have been some of my best teachers of theology. The final revisions to the manuscript were done while caring for a newborn; and without my mother-in-law, Tracy, taking on the daily work of laundry and washing dishes, those revisions would not have been possible. Whatever polish this book has is thanks to her. Zoi—I hope one day I will find the words. Cleo—welcome.